3/14/90

Fitness for Life

Childhood to Maturity

Fitness, Health & Nutrition was created by Rebus, Inc.
and published by Time-Life Books.

REBUS, INC.

Publisher: RODNEY FRIEDMAN
Editorial Director: CHARLES L. MEE JR.

Editor: THOMAS DICKEY
Senior Editor: LINDA EPSTEIN
Associate Editors: MARY CROWLEY, WILLIAM DUNNETT
Chief of Research: CARNEY W. MIMMS III
Copy Editor: ROBERT HERNANDEZ
Contributing Editors: JACQUELINE DAMIAN, JANE
SCHECHTER, SUSAN SILVERMAN

Art Director: JUDITH HENRY
Associate Art Director: FRANCINE KASS
Designer: SARA BOWMAN
Still Life and Food Photographer: STEVEN MAYS
Exercise Photographer: ANDREW ECCLES

Test Kitchen Director: GRACE YOUNG
Recipe Editor: BONNIE J. SLOTNICK

Time-Life Books Inc. is a wholly owned subsidiary of

TIME INCORPORATED

Founder: HENRY R. LUCE 1898-1967

Editor-in-Chief: JASON McMANUS
Chairman and Chief Executive Officer: J. RICHARD
MUNRO
President and Chief Operating Officer: N.J. NICHOLAS JR.
Editorial Director: RICHARD B. STOLLEY
President and Chief Executive Officer, THE TIME INC.
BOOK COMPANY: KELSO F. SUTTON
President and Chief Executive Officer, TIME INC.
BOOKS DIRECT: CHRISTOPHER T. LINEN

TIME-LIFE BOOKS INC.

Editor: GEORGE CONSTABLE

Executive Editor: ELLEN PHILLIPS
Director of Design: LOUIS KLEIN
Director of Editorial Resources: PHYLLIS K. WISE
Editorial Board: RUSSELL B. ADAMS JR., DALE M.
BROWN, ROBERTA CONLAN, THOMAS H. FLAHERTY, LEE
HASSIG, DONIA ANN STEELE, ROSALIND STUBENBERG
Director of Photography and Research: JOHN CONRAD
WEISER
Assistant Director of Editorial Resources: ELISE RITTER
GIBSON

President: JOHN M. FAHEY JR.
Senior Vice Presidents: ROBERT M. DeSENA, JAMES L.
MERCER, PAUL R. STEWART, JOSEPH J. WARD
Vice Presidents: STEPHEN L. BAIR, STEPHEN L.
GOLDSTEIN, JUANITA T. JAMES, ANDREW P. KAPLAN,
CAROL KAPLAN, SUSAN J. MARUYAMA, ROBERT H. SMITH
Supervisor of Quality Control: JAMES KING

Fitness for Life
Childhood to Maturity

Time-Life Books, Alexandria, Virginia

CONSULTANTS FOR THIS BOOK

David T. Lowenthal, M.D., Ph.D., a specialist in geriatric medicine, is Professor of Medicine, Science and Pharmacology and Director of the Geriatric Research, Education and Clinical Center at the University of Florida College of Medicine and the Veterans' Administration Medical Center in Gainesville, Florida. He has edited or coauthored more than 14 textbooks and has served as chairman of the medical committee for the Maccabiah Games, an International Olympic Committee-sanctioned event held in Israel.

Linda Scarpato-Place, M.S., is an ACSM-certified exercise physiologist at the 92nd Street YM-YWHA in New York City. She specializes in cardiac rehabilitation, stress testing, fitness testing and exercise prescription. She has been the director of Queens College's Children's Gymnastics and Movement Awareness programs for the past 10 years.

Diana Simkin, M.A., is an ASPO/ Lamaze childbirth educator. Currently the director of Family Focus, a center for expectant and new parents, she is the author of *The Complete Pregnancy Exercise Program,* and *The Complete Baby Exercise Program,* and the coauthor of *Preparation for Birth.*

Nutritional Consultants

Ann Grandjean, Ed.D., is Associate Director of the Swanson Center for Nutrition, Omaha, Neb.; chief nutrition consultant to the U.S. Olympic Committee; and an instructor in the Sports Medicine Program, Orthopedic Surgery Department, University of Nebraska Medical Center.

Myron Winick, M.D., is the R.R. Williams Professor of Nutrition, Professor of Pediatrics, Director of the Institute of Human Nutrition, and Director of the Center for Nutrition, Genetics and Human Development at Columbia University College of Physicians and Surgeons. He has served on the Food and Nutrition Board of the National Academy of Sciences and is the author of many books, including *Your Personalized Health Profile.*

For information about any Time-Life book please call 1-800-621-7026, or write:
Reader Information
Time-Life Customer Service
P.O. Box C-32068
Richmond, Virginia 23261-2068

Library of Congress Cataloging-in-Publication Data
Fitness for life
    (Fitness, health & nutrition; v. 19)
    Includes index.
    1. Exercise—Health aspects—Popular works. 2. Physical fitness—Popular works. I. Time-Life Books. II. Series: Fitness, health, and nutrition; vol. 19.
RA781.F57 1989   613.7'1   89-4487
ISBN 0-8094-6138-2
ISBN 0-8094-6139-0 (lib. bdg.)

This book is not intended as a substitute for the advice of a physician. Readers who are pregnant, or who have specific medical problems, should consult a physician about any suggestions made in this book. Readers who are beginning a program of strenuous exercise are also urged to consult a physician.

CONTENTS

Staying Active

Even as people have taken up fitness activities with unprecedented enthusiasm, it often seems that exercise programs are geared for people in the prime of life. Yet the benefits of exercise accrue to everyone, and in recent years exercise consultants and physiologists have directed more attention to fitness programs for children, for older adults and also for pregnant women, a more specialized — but still substantial — group. Expectant mothers, for example, are no longer being encouraged to take it easy. Rather, exercise can ease delivery and help a postpartum mother regain her shape more quickly. Children, it is often assumed, are active by nature. But, in fact, surveys show that a significant increase in obesity among children is attributable mainly to inactivity. One way to help children become more active is with exercises that are suited to their skill levels. Likewise, adults over 50, especially those who are not in good physical condition, require exercises of varying difficulty and intensity to help them regain their vigor. In addressing these special needs, this book can help to make fitness the lifelong pursuit that it should be.

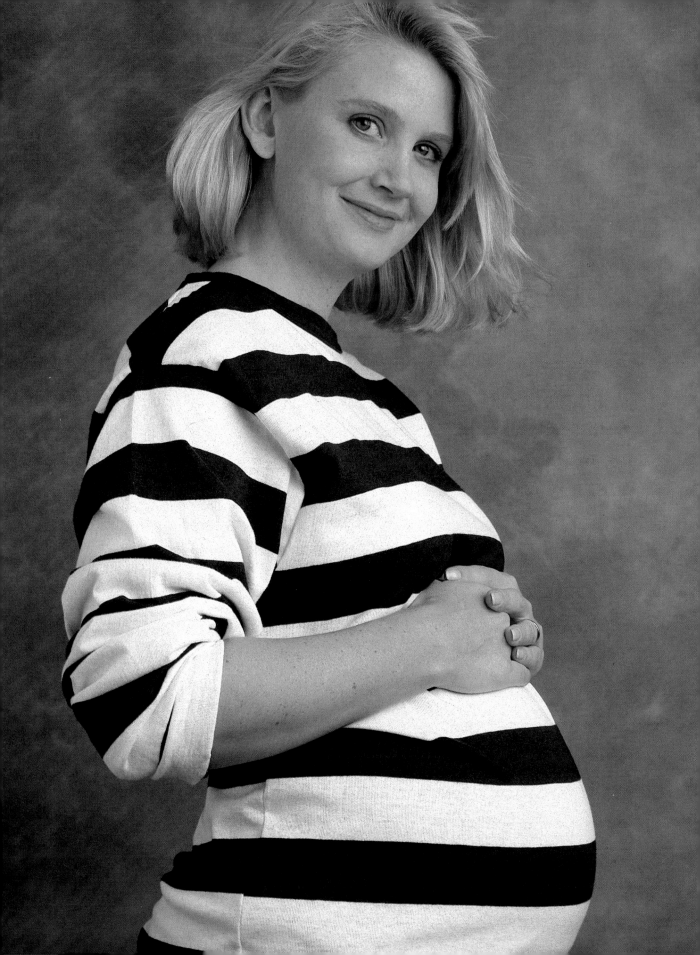

CHAPTER ONE

Childbearing

How to keep in shape during and after pregnancy

P hysicians have not always believed that exercise is beneficial for a pregnant woman: As recently as 20 years ago, expectant mothers were advised to counteract the physiological and hormonal stresses of pregnancy by taking it easy and staying off their feet as much as possible.

Now, however, most doctors encourage women with normal pregnancies to be active throughout the entire nine months. The right workout can increase energy, help prevent such pregnancy-related complaints as back strain and varicose veins and improve your body image; it can even ease your delivery.

In addition to providing benefits during pregnancy, an exercise program makes it easier to get back into shape after childbirth. The information in this chapter will help you to determine what kind and how much exercise to do, and the workout program shown on pages 14 to 47 illustrates safe and effective exercises for you to perform while you are pregnant and during the postpartum period.

Why should you exercise during pregnancy?

Exercise will help your body meet the demands of pregnancy and childbirth, as well as speed your muscles' recovery during the postpartum period. The American College of Obstetricians and Gynecologists (ACOG) cites three components of fitness that you should be concerned with during pregnancy: aerobic endurance, muscular strength and joint flexibility.

Pregnant women who perform endurance exercise can raise their aerobic capacity: One study reported an 18 percent increase in VO_2max in women who started an exercise program during their second trimester, while VO_2max declined by 4 percent in the non-exercising control group.

Muscle-strengthening and joint-flexibility exercises improve your body's muscular support system. This is especially important during pregnancy, when your musculature is required to withstand a great increase in weight. Movements that work the muscles of your abdomen, pelvis, perineum and hips can better help you to support this weight and improve your balance.

What kinds of exercise should you do during pregnancy?

There is a place for all types of exercise — aerobic, strengthening and flexibility — in an exercise program for pregnant women, so you will be able to continue most of your regular fitness activities. However, some types of exercise might need to be modified to accommodate your pregnancy. Impaired coordination and balance because of additional weight and variations in your center of gravity, as well as a greater risk of injury as a result of joint laxity, which is caused by hormone changes, can affect your performance and the safety of many fitness activities. In general, you should avoid any high-impact bouncing and twisting movements, as well as sports that might result in a blow to the abdomen. Specifically, competitive sports are not advised during pregnancy, nor are scuba diving, horseback riding and water and downhill skiing. Strength-training programs that involve weights should be undertaken only under supervision, so that progressive changes in posture can be monitored and routines adjusted accordingly. Be sure to consult with your physician, however, regarding any physical acitivity, since specific recommendations vary.

In addition to your usual fitness routines, you might want to include some exercises designed specifically to help your body adjust to the physiological demands of pregnancy, such as those on the following pages. For example, the pelvic floor exercise on page 21 will strengthen the muscles that support your enlarging uterus.

Is it safe to begin exercising when you are pregnant?

Yes. Because exercise will benefit your pregnancy, experts encourage you to start a gradual aerobic program of walking, bicycling or swimming, coupled with gentle muscle-strengthening and joint-flexibility exercises such as those shown in this chapter. You should not try to

Effects of Pregnancy

A pregnant woman has a smaller oxygen reserve than she had before her pregnancy, and the pressure in the thoracic region caused by her enlarged uterus makes it more difficult for her to breathe deeply. The result can be breathlessness or even hyperventilation during strenuous exercise. Also, because oxygen consumption (VO_2max) rises with body weight, an expectant mother's VO_2max is 15 to 30 percent higher than it was before her pregnancy. This means it will take more effort to do the same amount of exercise.

Pregnancy also stresses the cardiovascular system. Blood volume increases 30 to 45 percent, and the heart must work harder to pump the extra amount. The pulse rate may increase 10 to 20 beats per minute. As a result, it may be tiring for a pregnant woman to exercise as intensely as she did formerly.

The hormone relaxin causes a softening of the connective tissues, cartilage and tendons in a pregnant woman. This causes the joints to loosen, which may affect an expectant mother's ability to perform vigorous weight-bearing exercises. Also, the shift in her center of gravity affects a woman's balance.

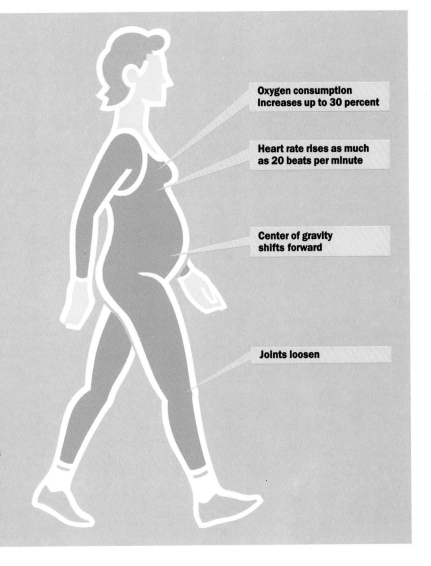

Oxygen consumption increases up to 30 percent

Heart rate rises as much as 20 beats per minute

Center of gravity shifts forward

Joints loosen

learn a new sport, however, or suddenly increase the intensity or amount of an exercise that you did before you were pregnant.

How does exercise affect the developing fetus?

Studies of fetal response to expectant mothers who exercise have recorded changes in fetal heart rate, temperature and metabolism. While in some circumstances, elevated fetal temperature can signify fetal distress, most studies have found no relationship between moderate exercise by the mother and the well-being of the newborn baby, its birth weight or its Apgar scores (measurements of the baby's physical condition and alertness evaluated at one and five minutes after birth). One study of 336 vigorous exercisers showed slightly lower newborn birth weights than did newborns of nonexercising women in a control group; however, this was not associated with a reduction in the newborns' Apgar scores or well-being. Indeed, another study of infants born to mothers who exercised regularly found significantly higher one-minute Apgar scores.

How much can you work out?
The ACOG guidelines for exercise during pregnancy and the postpartum period recommend working out at least three times a week at a moderate level of intensity. To determine your workout intensity, you should take your pulse periodically during exercise; while the optimal exercise rate will depend on the individual, the ACOG guidelines set an upper limit of 140 beats per minute, or between 60 and 70 percent of your maximum heart rate (220 minus your age). However, if you perceive your workout as too strenuous even at lower pulse rates, do not attempt to reach this level.

To avoid excessive increases in body temperature, which can be detrimental to a fetus, the ACOG guidelines also set a limit of 15 minutes per session on aerobic exercise. If you want to perform more than this, allow your pulse to drop back to its resting rate before you begin another 15-minute set. Avoid exercising in hot, humid weather. If your body temperature after exercise is 101 degrees F or higher, reduce your workout or exercise at a cooler time of day. The low-intensity stretching exercises shown in this chapter can be sustained for longer periods of time. All workout sessions should begin with a five-minute warm-up and finish with an equal cool-down period.

Stop exercising and notify your physician if at any time during physical activity you note the onset of any of the following symptoms: chest pain or headache, heart palpitations, shortness of breath, dizziness or fainting, nausea, uterine contractions or pain, leaking of amniotic fluid, vaginal bleeding, sudden swelling of the hands, ankles or face or a decrease in normal fetal movement. The ACOG does not recommend vigorous exercise if you have a history of three or more miscarriages, ruptured membranes, premature labor, incompetent cervix, bleeding or placenta previa, heart disease, or if you are expecting more than one baby.

Should you use exercise to control your weight during pregnancy?
No. Pregnancy is not a time to lose or even to control your weight unless your doctor tells you to do so. On average, pregnancy demands 300 additional calories daily to allow you to gain the ideal 24 to 34 pounds. Women who exercise during pregnancy should compensate for the extra calories burned by eating more. Experts recommend adding 200 to 300 extra calories for each 20- to 30-minute session of low-intensity aerobic exercise.

Are there exercises designed to relieve specific pregnancy-related complaints, such as backache and varicose veins?
The prenatal exercises provided in this chapter are specifically designed to help your body adjust to the burdens of pregnancy.

Exercise and Caesarean Sections

Percentage of Caesarean sections

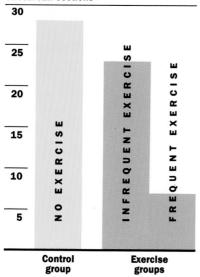

Among benefits that may be associated with exercise during pregnancy is a lower incidence of Caesarean sections. Although not all researchers have found such a correlation, one large-scale study of 845 pregnant women showed that exercise made a significant difference. Researchers divided the women into groups according to how often they engaged in a program of aerobic exercise and strength conditioning. Those who exercised most frequently — two to three times per week — had a markedly lower rate of Caesarean sections than women who exercised less or not at all.

Movements that strengthen the torso-supporting muscles of your back and abdomen, such as those on pages 22 and 26, will improve your posture and thereby relieve back strain and accompanying leg and hip problems. The exercises on pages 20 and 25 stretch the backs of your legs and help reduce leg cramps.

Some discomforts of pregnancy are allieviated by exercise in general. By improving your circulation, regular physical activity can ease varicose veins and help reduce the edema, or swelling, of your ankles and feet, a frequent complaint of expectant mothers. Exercise can also relieve digestive problems, such as gas and constipation. Exercisers in one study also reported improved sleep patterns.

Can exercise during pregnancy help prepare you for or ease labor and delivery?

To some extent, yes, although study results vary. Aerobic exercise can provide you with the endurance you will need if you have a long labor, and prenatal exercises targeted for your abdominals and thighs can allow you to take a more effective role in the actual delivery of your baby. However, conflicting results have been reported on the correlation between length of labor and exercise during pregnancy. One particular study did find that women who exercised during pregnancy spent less time recovering in hospitals when compared with those who were less active.

How soon after giving birth can you resume exercising, and which movements should you start with?

It takes six to eight weeks for your hormone and blood levels and cardiac output to return to their regular state after a normal vaginal delivery. However, exercise is not necessarily precluded during this period; indeed, it can speed recovery. Gentle stretching and strengthening exercises such as those on pages 28 to 41 can be performed as soon as you feel up to it. Experts say that moderate aerobic activity, with the exclusion of swimming, can be started in 10 to 14 days; you should avoid swimming until all vaginal bleeding has stopped. Do not pressure yourself to start strenuous exercise too soon, since your joints will still be loose for up to six weeks, making you more prone to injury. A recent study of female runners found they waited an average of five weeks before resuming training after childbirth. If you experience any discomfort during exercise, stop or slow down; if vaginal bleeding increases or becomes heavy, you should consult your physician immediately.

You should begin exercise more cautiously if you have had a Caesarean delivery; however, the way you feel should be your guide. A Caesarean section is major surgery, and recovery usually takes three to six weeks longer than the time required for recovery from a vaginal delivery. Do not exercise until your incision is healed or if it is painful. When you do start exercising, begin very slowly, and gradually increase the intensity of your workout over a two-month period.

Pregnancy/1

Exercising while you are pregnant is meant to help you feel as comfortable as possible with your added weight and continually changing body. The exercises here and on pages 16 to 27 are especially designed to tone and stretch your muscles without stressing your joints or taxing your cardiovascular system.

For your safety, there are some precautions you must take: Breathe steadily throughout your workout; do not hold your breath. As with any stretching and strengthening exercises, exhale during the movement that requires the most effort and inhale during the less active part. Since these exercises will not be demanding enough to make you gasp or hold your breath for the work phase, you should not have any problem in maintaining rhythmic, steady breathing. If your respiration becomes labored at any point, stop exercising and rest.

Perform your workout gently. Be careful not to stress your muscles or work too vigorously, especially when you begin the routine. Use the first exercises as warm-ups, to raise your muscle core temperature and get the blood flowing to the working tissues. The exercises that work your abdominal and leg muscles, shown on pages 18 to 23, are especially good preparation for the rigors of delivery. You will need toned abdominals to support your back and to help you push the baby out; strong legs mean you will not tire easily as you work through your labor.

SHOULDER CIRCLE Sit cross-legged with your fingertips on your shoulders, elbows close to your sides *(far left)*. Rotate your arms in front of you *(center)*, to the sides *(above)* and back to the starting position. Perform eight repetitions, then reverse direction.

SIDE STRETCH Sit cross-legged with your arms extended just below shoulder height. Reach to the left, allowing your left arm to rest on the floor *(far left)*. Return to the starting position *(center)*. Perform six repetitions, alternating sides *(above)*.

Pregnancy/2

FOOT WORK To tone your legs, sit erect with your legs extended and your arms at your sides. Point your toes *(top right)*, then flex your knees and feet as you raise and lower your legs *(right)*. Perform 10 repetitions.

TWIST To increase the flexibility of your back, sit cross-legged with your arms at your sides *(top left)*. Twist to the left from the waist, placing your left arm behind you for support *(left)*. Alternate sides and perform 12 repetitions.

Pregnancy/3

THIGH STRETCH Sitting with your legs bent and your arms extended behind you for support *(right)*, slowly squeeze and raise your buttocks off the floor to stretch and strengthen your hip and leg muscles *(far right)*. Perform four repetitions, then repeat on the other side.

HEAD LIFT To strengthen your upper abdominals, lie flat with your knees bent and your arms at your sides *(below)*. Exhale, contract your abdominals and raise your head and shoulders off the floor *(below right)*. Inhale to lower. Perform eight repetitions.

18

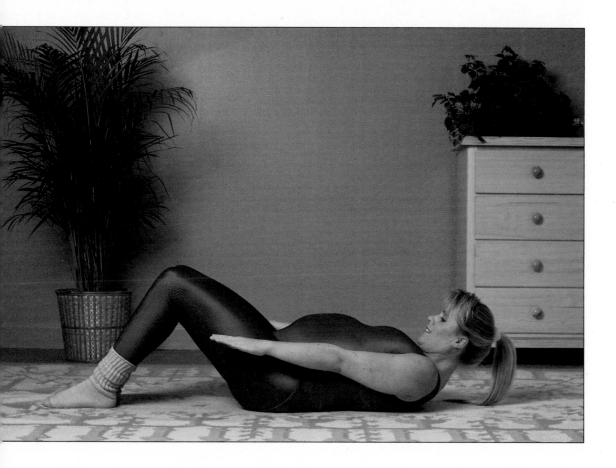

Pregnancy/4

LEG SWING Lie on your right side, lean on your right forearm and bend your right knee on the floor. Bend your left thigh toward your belly, extend it straight in front of you *(opposite top),* and swing it in a long arc to the back *(opposite center).* Bend your leg to bring it forward *(opposite bottom).* Be sure to keep your hips, shoulders and back aligned throughout the exercise. Perform 12 repetitions, then change sides.

PELVIC FLOOR EXERCISE Lie on your right side with your left knee bent and resting on a pillow for support *(below).* Tighten and lift the muscles of your pelvic floor — including your vaginal and anal sphincters — and hold the contraction for five seconds. Slowly release. Perform five repetitions. Turn onto your other side and repeat.

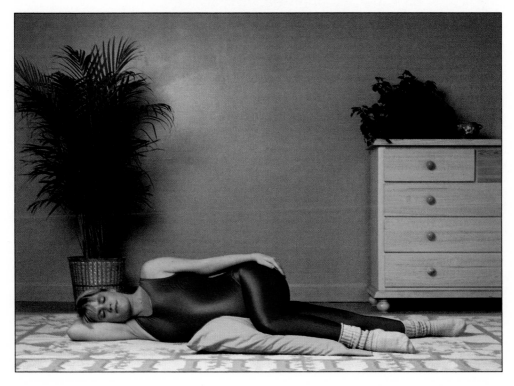

Pregnancy/5

OBLIQUE TUCK Lying on your back with your hands behind your head, rest your left foot on your bent right knee *(right)*. Contract your abdominals as you exhale and slowly lift your head and shoulders diagonally off the floor toward your left knee *(far right)*. Perform eight repetitions, then change sides.

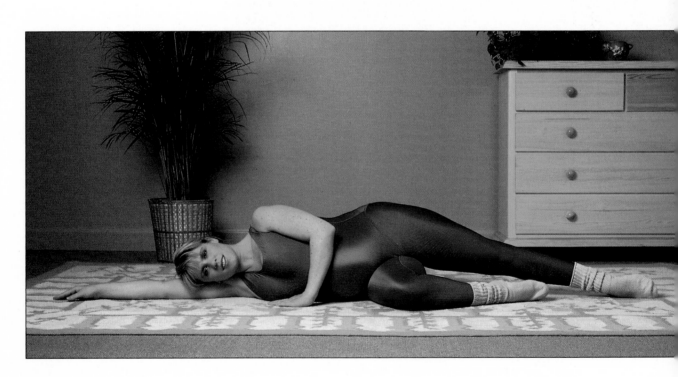

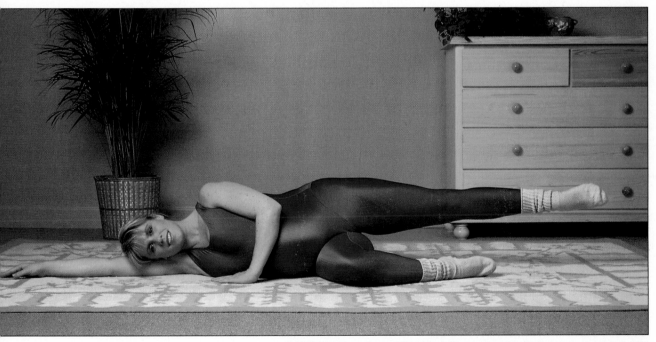

THIGH LIFT Lie on your right side, with your head resting on your extended right arm, your right knee bent on the floor and your left leg extended *(opposite above)*. Lift your left leg until it is parallel to the floor, to the height of your hip *(above)*. Perform 12 repetitions for each side.

Pregnancy/6

SINGLE-LEG STRETCH This whole-body stretch should be performed in one smooth movement. Sit with your right leg extended in front of you, your left arm at shoulder height extended behind you and the sole of your left foot against the inside of your right thigh *(inset, far left).* Reach upward with your left arm and turn to face front *(inset left).* Then relax and bend over your right thigh, lengthening your back and relaxing your elbows toward the floor *(left).* Unroll your spine and reach your left arm behind you. Perform eight repetitions, then change sides.

Pregnancy/7

CAT Visualize the way a cat stretches as you perform this exercise. Begin on all fours *(above)*. Round your back and contract your abdominal muscles *(above right)*. Release and lengthen your spine to a straight line. After six repetitions, stretch your buttocks to your calves, keeping your arms in front of you *(below right)*. Relax.

Postpartum/1

You can begin this postpartum exercise routine — with your doctor's permission — four to six weeks after delivery. Since women recover at different rates, it is important to check with your doctor before beginning this or any exercise program.

The many changes in your body after childbirth include some with consequences for exercise: You may find that you perspire a great deal as your body excretes the accumulated fluids of pregnancy. You may also feel much hotter than usual. If either condition affects you, take it easy when you do these exercises. Also, your ligaments and tendons, which loosened during pregnancy, are returning to their normal state. Vigorous exercise can stress them during this transition period, so work gently to avoid injury.

Do not force yourself to perform more than the number of repetitions you can do comfortably while maintaining proper form. As you regain your strength, you will be able to increase the number of repetitions.

For maximum strengthening and toning, perform these exercises daily. However, a minimum of three times per week is necessary to achieve actual fitness.

BODY CIRCLE To relax your back, neck and upper body, sit with your legs crossed and your hands on your knees. Bending from the waist, lean to your right *(far left, top)*, then forward *(left, top)*, to your left *(far left)* and back to the center *(left)*. Perform six repetitions in each direction.

WAIST STRETCH To tone your waist and hips, lie flat with your arms extended slightly below shoulder height and your knees raised toward your chest *(top)*. With your legs together, gently lower your knees to the floor on your left side *(above)*, keeping hands and shoulders on the floor if possible. Perform 20 repetitions, alternating sides.

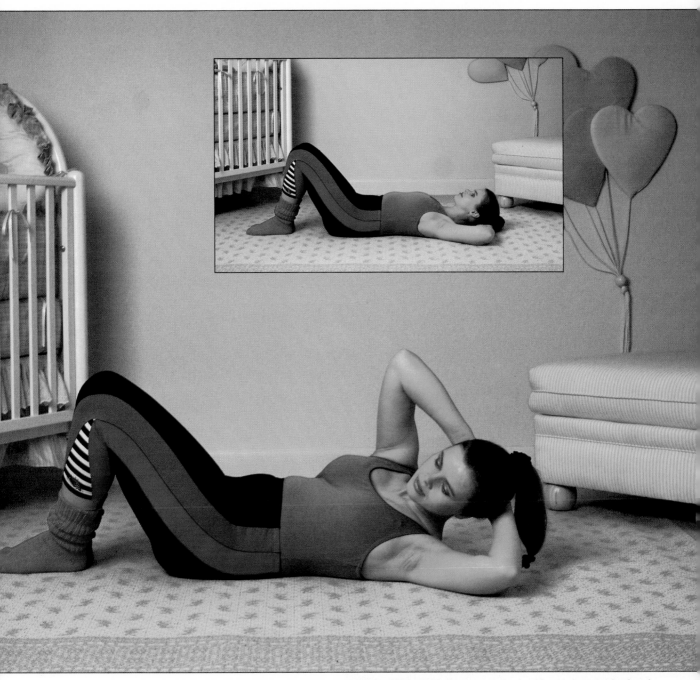

BELLY BUTTON ABS Lying on your back with your knees raised and feet flat on the floor, clasp your hands behind your head *(inset)*. Exhale. Contract your abdominals and lift your right shoulder off the floor on a diagonal toward your left knee *(above)*. Return, then lift your left shoulder. Perform 20 repetitions, alternating sides.

REVERSE SIT-UP Sit with your back straight, knees bent and arms in front of you *(top)*. Exhale. Contract your abdominals as you lower your back halfway to the floor *(above)*. Perform eight repetitions.

BACK MASSAGE To tone your inner thighs and abdominals, and to relax your lower back, lie on the floor with your knees a-part and the soles of your feet together *(top).* Contract your abdominals and slowly raise your back off the floor one vertebra at a time *(center and left).* Do not arch your back. Return to the starting position. Perform eight repetitions.

Postpartum/4

LEG STRETCH Lie on your back with your knees bent. Raise your left knee toward your chest *(right)*. Contract your abdominals and extend your left leg toward the ceiling *(center)*, and then flex them. Flex your foot and lengthen your leg as you slowly lower it to the floor *(far right)*. Keep the small of your back on the floor at all times. Perform 20 repetitions for each leg.

SPINE LIFT Lie on your back with your right knee bent and your right foot flat on the floor. Extend your left leg and point your toes. Exhale to raise your head and shoulders off the floor *(far left)*. Continue to contract your abdominals to raise your torso *(center),* and slide your hands along your left leg *(left).* Slowly lower your spine to the floor, holding the backs of your thighs for support. Throughout the movement, do not let your foot leave the floor. Perform five repetitions for each leg.

35

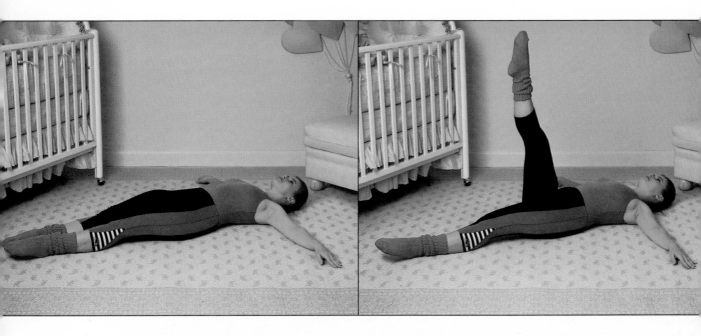

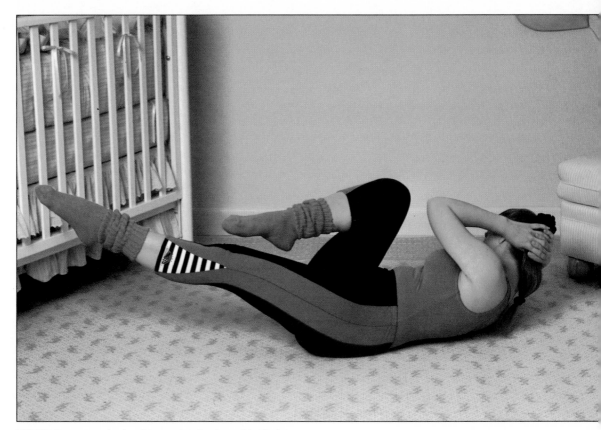

PISTON Lie on your back, with your hands clasped behind your head and your knees to your chest. Touch your left elbow to your bent right knee, keeping your left leg extended *(above)*. Alternate sides *(opposite);* perform 20 repetitions.

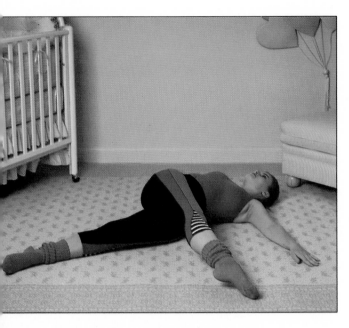

Postpartum/5

LEG CROSSOVER To stretch and tone your legs and waist, lie flat on your back with your arms spread just below shoulder level *(opposite)*. Raise your right leg to the ceiling, keeping it as straight as you can without lifting your left leg *(center)*. Bring your right leg over and across your body to touch the floor *(left)*. Lift your leg back to the center and slowly lower it to the floor. Repeat eight times for each leg, alternating sides.

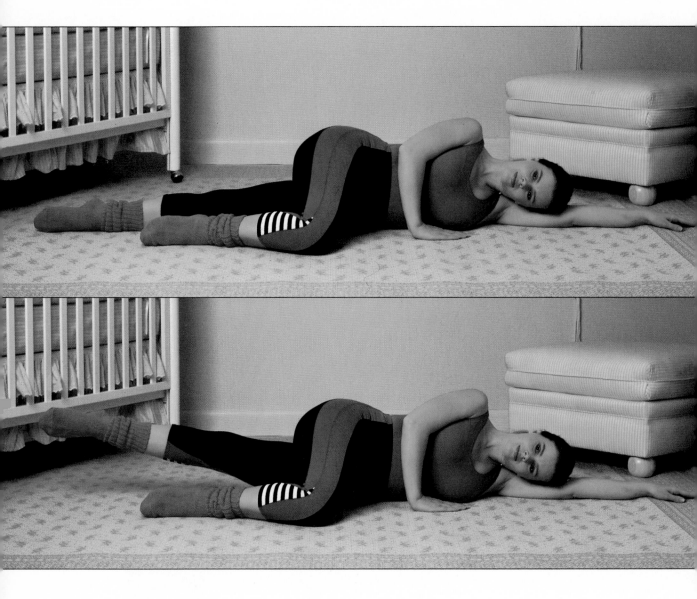

Postpartum/6

INNER THIGH RAISE To tone your inner thighs, lie on your left side with your head on your left arm. Bend your right leg, extend your left leg and point your toes *(top)*. Raise and lower your left leg *(above)*. Perform 20 repetitions for each leg.

HAMSTRING STRETCH Sit with your legs extended straight in front of you. Stretch forward over your legs, your feet pointed *(right)*. Slowly stretch your heels forward, flexing your feet *(bottom right)*. Repeat six times.

Postpartum/7

LEG SWING From a position on all fours, with your back rounded and your head tucked between your arms, bring your left knee toward your nose *(right)*. Then in one movement, extend your left leg back as you straighten your spine *(far right)*. Do not arch your back or raise your leg more than a little above hip height. Establish a smooth rhythm and perform 12 repetitions for each leg.

ARM PULSE Sit cross-legged with your arms straight out to the sides. Perform gentle pulsing movements for 16 repetitions in the four directions shown *(above, left to right):* palms facing behind you; palms facing front; palms down; palms up.

Mother and Baby/1

Y ou can include your baby in your postpartum exercise program, as the activities on the pages that follow show, both to give yourself a good workout, and to spend happy moments with your baby. The baby's weight will add to the resistance that your muscles must work against, and he or she will enjoy being held and hugged and gently moved about while you exercise.

As always, you must be sensitive to your baby's mood, to whether he or she is tired or cranky or tense. Exercises like the hip lift, shown on page 43, may help calm him down. If your baby is relaxed and playful, he might especially enjoy the movements on pages 42 and 45, which finish as you put your face close enough to kiss him. But you must also take your own feelings into account. Exercise with your baby when you feel like touching him and playing with him; if you are not in the mood to do so, the baby will sense this and may not respond well.

SHOULDER STRETCH With your back straight, sit cross-legged and clasp your hands behind your back *(top)*. Bend forward to kiss your baby's stomach *(above)*. Repeat eight times.

HIP LIFT With your baby resting on you, lie on your back with your knees bent and your feet about hip-width apart *(top)*. Slowly lift your pelvis off the floor *(above)*. Repeat eight times.

43

CALF RIDE Lie on your back with your knees raised and your legs together. Support your baby on your shins *(above)*. Holding your baby, and keeping your abdominals tight, raise your calves to a 45-degree angle *(above right)*. Repeat four times.

ROCKING HORSE With your back straight, knees bent and feet flat on the floor, sit with your baby resting on your shins *(right)*. Keeping your abdominals contracted, slowly roll onto your back, supporting your baby with both hands *(center and far right)*. Repeat eight times.

PUSH-UP On your hands and knees, with your back straight *(top right)*, lower your body until you can kiss your baby's stomach *(right)*. Perform 10 repetitions.

PLIE Holding your baby, stand with your feet hip-width apart and your toes pointed outward *(top).* Bend your knees and slowly lower your body. Tighten your inner thighs to straighten *(above).* Repeat 12 times.

ROCK-A-BYE Hold your baby facing downward with your hands clasped under her pelvis. Bend your left knee, straightening your right leg *(top right).* Shift to the center *(center),* then bend to the right *(right).* Repeat eight times in each direction.

TWIST Stand with your feet about hip-width apart, holding your baby on her back. Turn your torso to the left *(above left)*, and then to the right *(above)*. Twist from the waist, keeping your lower body stationary. Repeat eight times to each side.

CHAPTER TWO

Childhood

*Fun routines to build
coordination and confidence*

With their natural ebullience
and vast energy, children would seem to have no need for an exercise program. However, today's children are more sedentary than
previous generations. Two recent wide-ranging studies of 13,000
students from the first through the twelfth grades found that fitness
levels were unsatisfactory for a great number of children. Nearly half
of them did not get enough exercise, in or out of school, to develop
healthy hearts and lungs. Younger children have been less widely
studied, but one group of researchers discovered that many of the
three- to five-year-olds in a small study could not touch their toes, a
standard test of flexibility. Concerned, health-conscious parents are
increasingly aware of the need to encourage their children to become
more physically active. Developing an exercise habit early can be the
cornerstone of a lifelong commitment to fitness. Because the exercises are specifically suited for children at various stages of their
motor development, they are challenging without being discouraging.

Do children really need an exercise program or are they active enough naturally?

Some children appear to be perpetual-motion machines, tearing around the playground or running rather than walking whenever they can. But a number of nationwide studies suggests that our traditional view of childhood as a time of lively, nonstop activity may not be the whole story. For example, the President's Council on Physical Fitness and Sports has found that 40 percent of boys aged six to 15 cannot touch their toes; and 40 percent of boys and 70 percent of girls aged six to 17 are unable to perform more than a single pull-up. In another study, one-third of the boys and half of the girls aged six to 12 failed to run a mile in less than 10 minutes. What is more, today's children are significantly fatter than the children of a decade or two ago *(see the chart on page 53)*. Inactivity is seen as playing a key role in causing the weight gain.

Although most experts believe that normal play activity should be enough to keep children fit, trim and healthy, there is now some discrepancy in what constitutes normal play. Many children now spend more time with video games than they do playing tag. Parents often drive their children places rather than let them walk or ride their bikes. And, of course, many children spend a great deal of time sitting passively in front of a TV. One study has found that 32 percent of fourth-graders watch six or more hours of television a day; the Nielsen organization estimates that the average child spends 25 hours per week watching TV.

As a result of these findings, a number of national organizations, including the President's Council on Physical Fitness and the American Academy of Pediatrics, have recently warned that to attain an adequate level of fitness, children must become more active.

Does physical education in school provide exercise for children?

On average, schools today offer fewer physical education classes than they did in the past. Only 10 percent of the nation's elementary schools require daily gym classes, and some students get as little as one hour of physical education per week; the average is two to three hours. As a result, the typical student gets more than 80 percent of his or her physical activity outside school, either through community organizations or in informal play.

Even in school districts that mandate frequent or daily physical education, there is no guarantee that gym classes will make a child fit. Most school programs emphasize such sports as soccer, football, basketball and baseball. While these activities may be fun, they are primarily games of skill, speed and agility. More important to a child's overall fitness is a program of aerobic activity that builds the cardiovascular system — biking, running or swimming, for example.

Is there an advantage to a formal exercise program?

Everyone agrees that children need exercise. But the question of just

How a Child Develops

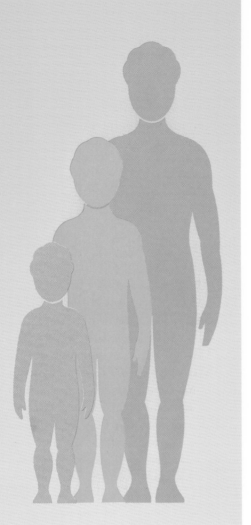

NEUROMUSCULAR SYSTEM

Progressive development to the age of sexual maturity, at a gradual pace conducive to building coordination, agility and motor skills; boys do not build significant muscle mass from training until adolescence.

CARDIOVASCULAR SYSTEM

Aerobic capacity increases gradually, then rises dramatically at puberty; small children tolerate endurance exercise well but do not derive the same cardiovascular benefits —called the training effect— that adults and adolescents do.

MUSCLES

Rapid growth in muscle mass to age seven, followed by slower development until the growth spurt of adolescence; intensive strength training prior to this may be inadvisable.

BONES

Skeletal development can continue to age 18 or later; regular exercise throughout childhood results in denser, stronger bones.

what constitutes appropriate exercise for children of different ages is complex. The experts simply do not have all the answers, especially regarding very young children. Despite the lack of consensus, exercise classes for preschoolers are becoming more popular, many of them offering aerobic dance and structured activity on playground equipment. Research on the aerobic needs of preschoolers is sketchy, and there is no evidence that formal exercise programs advance a young child's fitness level. The American Academy of Pediatrics has stated that classes for children under the age of three do absolutely nothing to enhance growth and development. It is better just to let your toddlers play, or to play and exercise with them.

Still, some parents might find an exercise program a good way to pry a child away from the TV and begin some physical activity. If you want to enroll young child in an exercise group, many experts advise looking for one that emphasizes creative movement. Very young children are just learning motor skills and coordination, so a program built around agility and the fun of movement will be more effective than aerobics. In fact, to guard against the risk of injuring young muscles and bones, some physiologists advise introducing children to a formal aerobics routine only when they reach the fifth grade.

Are organized sports a good idea for children?

Some children are athletically inclined and, for them, playing on a team can be an effective way to exercise. There are a few pitfalls to avoid, however. First, not all sports are equally good conditioners. Football and baseball, for example, involve intense bursts of activity interspersed with a lot of rest time. So even if your child plays on a team, encourage him or her to walk, ride a bike or swim — activities that will condition the cardiovascular system and provide enjoyment throughout a lifetime.

Also, support your child's venture into sports without placing an undue emphasis on winning. That kind of pressure, often called Little League Syndrome, can create anxiety, diminish self-esteem and lead to competitive stress, which occurs when a child perceives that the demands of the game are greater than his or her abilities to meet them. Of course, some competitive stress is intrinsic to playing sports, but parents can ensure that their child will not be overly pressured by taking a positive approach and praising the child for performance and effort, not results. One recent study found that children who were praised and who felt they met their parents' expectations enjoyed sports far more than those who did not. Psychologists believe that the minimum-pressure approach is especially crucial for preadolescents. With this age group, the emphasis should be on the fun of playing. Only after age 14 are children ready for more intense training.

Is vigorous aerobic exercise advisable for children?

Children should be encouraged to participate in moderately brisk aerobic activities, and running is a wise choice, except for the very young. Physiologically, children are surprisingly adaptable to endurance exercise even if they are not in top condition. Although their absolute oxygen uptake (VO_2max) is low, their aerobic capacity relative to weight exceeds that of adults. In addition, children perceive prolonged exercise as less tiring than adults do.

If your child is interested in running, make sure the program he or she undertakes is gradual and well supervised. Children should wear well-fitting running shoes, and warm up and cool down properly to minimize the risk of injury *(see pages 54-55 and 60-61)*.

Can exercise injure young bones and muscles?

For preadolescents, there is a risk of overuse injuries when exercise is especially intense or lengthy — long-distance running, for example. Children also have less efficient heat-dissipation mechanisms than adults do, which limits their ability to sweat. This is another reason to use extreme caution in any long-distance aerobic activities. For example, you can guard against heat stress by making sure that young runners drink plenty of water.

Should children undertake weight training?

Little research has been done on the effect of weight training on prepubescent children, but one recent study suggests it can be safe as long as the exercise is well supervised by experienced trainers. Eighteen boys of an average age of eight enrolled in the study, which involved working out on hydraulic-resistant machines under close supervision for 14 weeks. All the subjects recorded strength gains, and only one boy sustained an injury — a shoulder strain. The researchers concluded that a carefully monitored weight-training program would not adversely affect bone and muscle growth.

However, most exercise physiologists believe that working out with weights has the potential for injury. They recommend that weight training be postponed until a child is at least 10, and only done with experienced trainers, not parents or coaches.

Can exercise habits prevent health problems later in life?

Typically, an active child who exercises regularly will grow into an adult who continues a program of physical activity. And, in countless studies, regular exercise has been found to prevent health problems, including coronary heart disease, obesity and some forms of cancer.

From this perspective, health professionals are especially concerned about how low levels of fitness in children might affect their long-range health. The problems of inactivity and obesity are two major concerns. In addition, researchers have recently uncovered an alarming trend toward elevated blood cholesterol levels in a considerable number of children: in one major study, 24 percent of 4,000 children surveyed had this condition, which is considered a risk factor for heart disease in adults. But no one knows just what these results mean for the children's future disposition to illness.

Fitness also plays a part in a child's life in a host of less dramatic ways. Strong muscles, particularly the abdominals, guard against lower back pain, a problem that afflicts eight out of 10 people at some point in their lives. Regular exercise reduces stress and promotes a sense of well-being. And studies show that children who are physically active learn better and have more energy for their schoolwork.

How important is family example in building fitness in children?

Exercise physiologists believe that the example of parents has a profound effect on children — that fitness is a habit that can be learned at home, much like table manners or personal hygiene. Besides setting a good example by means of their own exercise habits, parents can exercise with their children; a number of parent-child routines are shown in this chapter. Finally, parents can encourage after-school activities and limit TV viewing.

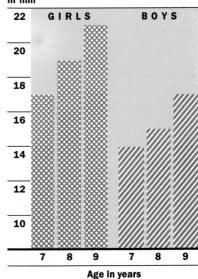

Childhood Obesity: On the Rise

Skinfold measurement in mm

■ 1980s
■ 1960s

The fact that American children are becoming fatter is suggested by two surveys of 4,000 elementary schoolchildren conducted in a 20-year interval. Researchers took skinfold measurements in a number of body locations, then added the figures to get the totals shown in the chart. This technique, which is a standard test of obesity, disclosed that children surveyed in 1980 were significantly heavier than those measured in 1960. The researchers concluded that the children's weight gain was caused by a lack of exercise.

53

Parent and Child/1

As children grow, they are continually learning about the way their bodies move in their environment. This increasing spatial and body awareness, along with foot- and hand-to-eye coordination, are the most important movement skills to be developed through the fifth year of life.

The exercises shown on this and the following 19 pages are specifically designed for children aged three to five to provide an enjoyable introduction to a lifetime of fitness activities. The warm-ups — the Airplane, Toe Game, and Tall/Small, for example — will also enhance and maintain children's flexibility, which is at its highest level in this age group. Movement exercises like Animal Games and Worm Rolls benefit the cardiovascular system and teach coordination. Strengtheners like Push/Pull, See-Saw and push-ups will contribute to the development of strong bones and muscles.

Keep in mind that these exercises should be fun, above all. Very young children have short attention spans, and you will find that a creative, unpressured atmosphere, a playful approach to fitness, will succeed best. For this reason, no set number of repetitions is given for these exercises. Perform them as many times and for as long as you and your child enjoy them.

AIRPLANE Stand facing your child, holding hands, with his arms extended *(inset, top)*. Pretend that your arms are airplane wings, and bend them first to one side *(inset, bottom)*, and then to the other side *(opposite)*.

54

Parent and Child/2

PUSH/PULL Face your child and hold his hands with his arms straight up *(far left)*. Using his right deltoid and triceps muscles, your child pushes against your left arm *(center)*. At the same time, you push back; your child resists your arm pressure with his triceps. Alternate sides *(left)*.

IN/OUT Stand facing your child, holding hands *(far left)*. Rhythmically stretch his arms out to his sides, parallel to his shoulders *(center)*, then back to the starting position *(left)*, to stretch his shoulders and chest.

Parent and Child/3

STANDING SQUAT Stand facing your child, holding hands *(inset left)*. Your child pretends to sit on an imaginary chair without moving his feet *(left)* to strengthen and tone his quadriceps and buttocks.

CALF STRETCH Stand side by side with your legs spread. Twist your torsos toward each other. Your child leans forward and twists, bending his knee as you push against his shoulders. He pushes against your leg to stretch his calf *(top right)*. He changes legs and repeats the stretch with his other calf *(right)*.

TOE GAME To stretch your child's legs, sit opposite and next to each other with your legs extended. Say, "Flex," as you flex your feet *(above left)*. Say, "Point," as you point your toes *(above)*.

PIKE / TUCK To stretch your hips, knees and shoulders, say, "Pike," as you raise your arms toward the ceiling *(above left)*. Say, "Tuck," as you bend your knees and tuck your head between them *(above)*.

TALL / SMALL Stand facing your child, and ask, "How tall can you get?" as you both reach toward the ceiling and stand on your toes *(inset)*. Ask, "How small can you get?" as you drop to the floor and curl up *(above)*.

61

Parent and Child/5

PUSH-UP Facing each other, support yourself with your hands placed shoulder-width apart and your knees bent *(above)*. Lower until you are flat on the floor, head to head *(above opposite)*. Rise by pushing up.

SEE-SAW Sit facing your child, holding hands, with his bent knees against your calves *(right)*. Your child leans back until just his shoulders touch the floor *(center)*. Then he comes forward as you lean back *(far right)*.

SEAL WALK Your child lies on his stomach *(top),* and moves across the
floor, alternately reaching forward with his arms and shoulders, dragging
his legs as he progresses *(above).*

Animal Games/1

I mitating the locomotive movements of animals is not only fun for children, but it also develops their awareness of how their bodies move.

The Seal Walk and Inch Worm on this page and the Elephant Walk on page 68 are all strengthening exercises for your child's arms and shoulders, which are significantly weaker than the rest of his body. The Crab Walk on page 67 uses your child's quadriceps and buttocks in addition to his biceps, triceps and shoulders. The Kangaroo Jump on page 66 is primarily a lower body movement.

All five exercises are excellent for teaching your child to coordinate his upper and lower body as well as his right and left sides. If he does these exercises in succession for 15 minutes or longer, he will derive aerobic benefits as well.

INCH WORM Your child bends forward so that his hands touch the floor as close as possible to his feet (1). He takes two steps with his hands without moving his feet (2,3). Then he takes two steps forward with his feet without moving his hands (4), and continues.

KANGAROO JUMP Your child leans forward with his knees slightly bent and his arms behind him *(inset)*. When he starts to jump, he moves his arms forward to increase his momentum *(above)*.

66

Animal Games/2

CRAB WALK Your child lies on a mat on his back. Supporting his weight with his arms and legs *(right)*, he walks backward by moving his left arm and right leg *(center)*, and then his right arm and left leg *(bottom)*.

Animal Games/3

ELEPHANT WALK From a standing position, your child bends from the waist until his hands touch the floor *(right)*. He takes a step forward by moving his right arm and right leg simultaneously *(center)*. Then he moves his left arm and leg *(bottom)*.

Animal Games/4

WORM ROLL This whole-body stretch begins with your child lying flat on his back with both arms extended above his head (1). Then he rolls to his side (2), face down (3), and on to his other side (4).

BUG ROLL For this easier version of the Worm Roll, your child clasps his knees. He begins the exercise on his back (1), rolls to the side (2), then face down (3), and on to his other side (4).

Vault and Punch

The object of this exercise is for your child to run toward you, jump into the center of a hoop (or a target spot marked on the floor with tape) and then leap up to dislodge a ball from your hands. This is lots of fun, of course, but the point is that he uses his gross motor skills (running and jumping) at the same time as his fine-motor ability to focus on the ball and aim well.

Learning the necessary eye-to-hand coordination is easier if you break the movement into a series of components: Your child should first walk to you, then jump into the hoop and finally knock the ball out of your hands. Make sure you hold the ball within his reach so he does not become frustrated or lose interest. As he becomes more proficient, you can make the exercise more challenging by raising the ball higher.

Stand facing your child at a distance of about 15 feet and hold the ball over the center of the hoop (1). Say, "Go." Your child runs toward you (2). At the last step before the hoop, he jumps up from one foot, lands on both feet in the center (3), then jumps up again to knock the ball out of your hands (4).

4

Older Children/1

The flexibility so characteristic of young children begins to decline as they mature. Performing the stretches shown on pages 76 to 80 will help your child to maintain flexibility as his or her strength begins to develop.

From the ages of six to 10, children's overall muscularity increases considerably. And one goal of exercise during this growth period, in addition to maintaining flexibility, is to enhance strength. Exercises like the Bridge (page 81) and push-ups (page 83), for example, are strengtheners for the upper body and the abdominals. Both these areas can be underutilized even by active children who run frequently.

The other important stage of development for children in this age group is hand-to-eye coordination. The Zigzag Game and Balloon Volleyball on pages 85 and 86 will increase your child's ability to catch and throw, to jump and land accurately, and to change direction quickly without losing his or her balance.

HIGH JUMP Beginning from a crouch, have your child jump up as high as he can, lifting his arms above his head when he takes off, to increase his momentum *(left)*.

SKI JUMP Have your child start with his arms at his sides with his elbows bent as if he were holding ski poles. With his feet together and his knees bent, he jumps to the left while turning his upper body to the right *(above left)*, and then to the right while turning his upper body to the left *(left)*.

PIKE STRETCH Your child should sit with her legs extended, her back straight and her head and neck aligned. She flexes her feet and raises her arms straight above her head *(top)*, then she bends from the waist to touch her toes, holding the stretch for 20 seconds *(above)*.

MOUNTAIN CLIMB From a modified push-up position, have your child support herself on her hands, extending her left leg behind her and bending her right knee under her chest *(opposite, top)*. She changes legs while supporting her weight on her hands *(opposite)*.

Older Children/3

STRADDLE STRETCH Your child should sit with her legs spread and her arms extended over her head *(inset, opposite)*. As she lowers her arms to shoulder height, she bends first to the left *(inset, left)*, and then to the right *(opposite)* to stretch her hamstrings and obliques.

BUTTERFLY STRETCH Sitting with her knees bent and feet together, your child should grasp her ankles *(top)*. She bends from the waist to touch her head to her feet *(above)*, keeping her head and back aligned and her elbows pressed against the insides of her knees.

Older Children/4

ROPE CLIMBING Keeping both feet on the floor, have your child reach as high as she can to grab an imaginary rope, stretching alternately with her left arm *(right)*, and then with her right *(below)*.

BRIDGE Lying on her back with her knees raised and feet flat, your child should place her hands next to her ears, palms down *(top)*. Using her arm and leg muscles, she lifts herself off the floor as high as she can and holds the stretch for at least 10 seconds *(above)*.

81

QUARTER SIT-UP Have your child lie on his back with his hands by his ears, bending his knees and raising his legs until parallel to the floor *(above, opposite)*. He contracts his abs and lifts his shoulders to touch his elbows to his knees *(above)*.

PUSH-UP With his hands shoulder-width apart, your child should support his weight with his arms straight *(above, opposite)*. He lowers himself to the floor, keeping his back straight, and then pushes himself up *(above)*.

Older Children/6

ZIGZAG COURSE To set up the course, place five hoops as shown *(below)*, approximately 10 feet apart. Your child enters the course from hoop 1, then moves to the center hoop to perform an activity *(see caption opposite)* before moving to hoop 2 *(above left)* and back to the center and so on. All activity takes place in the center hoop. The game is over when your child completes the course, or at the end of a specified time.

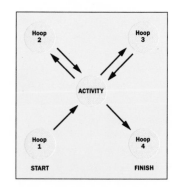

ZIGZAG GAME The activities your child should perform in the center hoop include tossing the ball overhead *(above center)*, dribbling the ball behind him *(far left)*, and bouncing the ball off his knee *(left)*. Design more difficult activities as your child's skill develops.

Older Children/7

BALLOON VOLLEYBALL Use a balloon to slow the game of volleyball for your children: *Bump:* He should hit the balloon with his lower forearm using a small upward movement *(above)*. The force is increased when your child first bends at the hips and knees and follows through by extending his legs fully. *Set:* She should set herself to return the balloon with her hands cocked back, palms up and fingers tensed *(right)*. *Overhead serve:* He should throw the balloon up in front of him with his less-dominant hand, then hit the balloon with the heel of his dominant hand as it falls, and step forward to add force to his serve *(far right)*.

CHAPTER THREE

Over Fifty

Exercises to maintain muscle, flexibility and vigor

M ost older Americans believe that their need for exercise declines with age, but this is not true. Just as for younger people, regular exercise provides numerous physiological and psychological benefits for individuals over 50 that cannot be gained in any other way. Only a regular program of exercise allows older people to maintain, or even to increase, their strength, stamina and flexibility.

Weak muscles, reduced endurance and limited flexibility are not inevitable. In fact, many of the deleterious changes in your body that are supposedly due to aging are actually the outcome of sedentary living. By staying active, you can maintain flexibility and endurance as well as your aerobic capacity, even into the last decades of your life. If you have been inactive, you can take action to improve your physical fitness. This requires adopting a program of regular aerobic exercise in addition to exercises designed to enhance your strength and flexibility. This chapter provides routines for people over 50, to get them started on safe, lifelong conditioning workouts.

Must you lose your fitness if you are over 50?
To some extent, yes. Your maximum heart rate declines, and your lungs and blood vessels become less elastic as you get older. From ages 30 to 80, the resting cardiac index declines by 20 to 30 percent, and an 80-year-old typically has about 40 percent of the breathing capacity of a 30-year-old. Because your heart and lungs supply less oxygen to your tissues, your sense of well-being and vitality diminishes as you age. You tire more easily.

How does aging affect strength and flexibility?
Muscle strength for both men and women reaches its peak between the ages of 20 and 30 — when muscle mass is at its greatest. After 30, the number of your muscle cells stops increasing, and by age 50, the cells begin to deteriorate. Older people's muscles are less able to store glycogen, the carbohydrate fuel for activity; therefore, all other conditions — such as the amount of training — being equal, older people do not have as much muscle endurance as younger people do. The muscle tissue of older adults contains more fat and collagen — the material that connective tissue is made of — and it is less able to contract than younger people's muscle tissue. As a result, the risk of injury increases as you age.

Morning stiffness is a very common problem of aging, since as you get older, chemical links called side chains form around muscle tissue during the night or when you are sedentary, making muscle contractions more difficult. Even active people notice morning stiffness beginning in midlife.

As a result of aging, the connective tissues such as tendons and ligaments, which connect muscles to bones and bones to bones, respectively, show a decrease in blood supply. The risk of tendon rupture increases where the amount of blood is most reduced. And the point at which a tendon extends into a bone can become problematic, since bone material, to which the tendon anchors, is thinner. Ligaments harden with age and become increasingly liable to tear. And collagen in the connective tissues has a tendency to contract with age, unless it is stretched regularly. Therefore, if you do not deliberately use your joints in their full range of motion, they will tighten.

In fact, the most frequent complaint of older people, according to doctors, concerns the joints: An estimated 57 percent of people over 55 suffer from a loss of joint mobility. A study at the Johns Hopkins Medical School made clear that the difficulty lies primarily in the connective tissues and muscles, not in the bones.

To what extent is loss of flexibility caused by arthritis?
Painful stiffness and swelling of the joints — osteoarthritis — is the most common joint complaint of older women. It may be the result of misuse or overuse of the joints, but since research shows that most people over age 40 have some signs of this condition (only about half of them suffer symptoms), it may simply be a result of aging.

How Fitness Slows Aging

AEROBIC ENDURANCE

- Maintains optimal cardiovascular functioning, which may guard against heart disease and other health problems
- Raises HDL, "good," cholesterol
- Burns calories and helps to maintain optimal body weight and composition
- Reduces psychological stress

STRENGTH AND FLEXIBILITY

- Delays the loss of strength and muscle mass that occurs with aging
- Maintains muscle tone and joint range of motion, which help to prevent backaches and joint disorders
- Facilitates balance
- Slows bone shrinkage and weakening, which may prevent osteoporosis

Osteoarthritis affects the cartilage at the ends of bones. Cartilage is a spongy material made mostly of water. When your bones must bear weight, the cartilage becomes compressed, absorbing shocks by secreting a lubricant that lessens friction between joint surfaces. As you age, osteoarthritis causes your cartilage to dehydrate, thin and develop little fractures. If, in addition, muscle side chains and contracted collagen restrict your range of motion, a limited area of cartilage receives extra stress, which causes more deterioration.

Can exercise really help slow down these effects of aging?

Maybe. The best way to prevent pain from osteoarthritis, for example, is to keep physically fit. Gentle stretches and strengthening movements, such as those shown in this chapter, can help maintain flexibility, and even enhance it. A study conducted at the University of Wisconsin found that women over the age of 70 improved the range of motion in their necks, hips and backs by more than 25 percent after only 12 weeks of flexibility exercises.

If you exercise, research has shown that you can maintain or even gain muscle mass as you age, though you cannot get quite the benefits that younger people do. In California, for example, a study found that elderly people could attain a percentage of strength improvement comparable to younger adults. At West Virginia University, a group of women aged from 50 to 63 who walked or participated in aerobic dance programs for six months improved their muscle strength and endurance significantly. A study conducted with runners found that their musculoskeletal disabilities developed more slowly than in people who did not run.

Aerobic exercise improves cardiovascular fitness, respiratory capacity and muscular endurance. It can also lower blood pressure and cholesterol levels, and aid in weight control. A study at Western New Mexico University showed that postmenopausal women who engaged in high-intensity exercise increased their cardiovascular fitness significantly. Research reported in the *Journal of Gerontology* on three age groups of walkers showed that aerobic capacity is not necessarily correlated with age: Some fast walkers in the oldest group were as fit as those in younger groups. (For this reason, the routine shown in this chapter is meant to accompany regular aerobic workouts.)

What is osteoporosis, and what effect does exercise have on it?
Bone, not including the marrow, consists of water, connective tissue and minerals, mostly calcium phosphate. Although its mineral content makes it hard, bone is living tissue that weakens gradually with age. This weakening, or demineralization, occurs when bones cannot absorb calcium from the bloodstream; they atrophy and become porous and brittle, making them very prone to fracture. When it is severe, this condition is called osteoporosis, which may be an inevitable consequence of aging. Osteoporosis affects 24 million Americans. Perhaps because of hormonal differences, women's bones generally weaken sooner than men's do, and four times more women over the age of 50 are affected by osteoporosis.

Numerous studies have shown that exercise reduces bone mineral loss in older people, and inactivity greatly accelerates it. Although the mechanism is not known, research indicates that bones respond to the pull of gravity when you perform weight-bearing exercise like walking, bicycling, jogging, and to muscle contraction, by increasing in density. A study found that bone mineral mass was greater in postmenopausal women aged 50 to 62 who exercised for a year than in a nonexercising control group. Similar results have been obtained in studies of older men: It is clear that exercise strengthens bones.

Falling is more dangerous for older people because their bones have weakened. And since your ability to maintain your balance is compromised as you age — your muscle strength is diminished, your vision is not as sharp and there are changes in your brain cells and blood pressure — you are somewhat more likely to fall.

Can exercise preserve your sense of balance?
It can, to some degree. A study done in New York showed that balance requires interaction between what you see and what you sense with the proprioceptors in your inner ear — stimuli that are linked in the cerebral cortex. As you age, the links in the brain can break

down, possibly as a result of minor strokes. Adequate muscle strength and flexibility are required to counteract your diminished ability to balance, and exercise makes you stronger, more flexible and better able to catch yourself if you do begin to fall. In addition, exercise can retard arthritis, which can pull posture out of line, also making you more liable to fall. This is a serious problem: More than 200,000 Americans suffer broken hips every year.

What constitutes a sound exercise program?

Regular aerobic workouts performed for a minimum of three times per week for 20 minutes, plus five minutes each of warm-up and cool-down, totaling 30 minutes per session, is optimal for maintaining cardiovascular fitness. However, studies show that any amount of physical activity is better than none.

If you are aerobically fit, you will find the stretches that keep your joints flexible considerably easier to perform than you would if you were out of shape. And conversely, being flexible and having joints that can move comfortably throughout their full range of motion makes aerobic exercise not only more pleasant but much safer.

Is it ever too late to begin exercising?

Clearly, it is never too late: After you have consulted with your physician and received permission to begin an exercise program, you will find that even if you have been sedentary for years, you can become physically fit. A study at San Diego State University in California showed that of three groups of men between the ages of 45 and 55, those who had rarely exercised were able to achieve fitness levels nearly comparable to those who had exercised regularly for 10 years. At the conclusion of the study, aerobically speaking, the men were functionally younger than they had been at the start.

What is the safest way to get started?

If you have never participated in an exercise program, or if you have been sedentary for a long time, your initial conditioning regimen should be limited to a period of approximately 12 minutes of aerobic exercise (after your warm-up), then gradually increased. To be cautious, perform this initial conditioning period for four to six weeks.

The basic routine provided in this chapter serves as a solid foundation to begin with. As you develop your flexibility and stamina, you can progress to the more difficult versions of the illustrated exercises or increase your repetitions.

Keep in mind that your workouts should not cause you pain. If so, you are more likely to be injured, or to stop exercising altogether, than the person who pushes himself less and proceeds slowly. The point of exercising for increased longevity is to improve your quality of life — to make your life more worth living because you are capable of being more active. Enjoyable workouts that increase your vitality should be a welcome addition to your everyday life.

The Upper Body/1

As you get older and your joints are less flexible, performing stretching exercises becomes increasingly important. You can test your range of motion by standing in front of a mirror and raising your arms toward the ceiling. The more vertical you can hold them, the more flexible you are.

Turn sideways, clasp your hands behind your back and move them away from your body as far as you can. If your range of motion is good, you should be able to move them at least 10 inches away from your back, with your hands raised at least to waist level.

An additional test is the palm twist: With your arms at your sides and your palms facing behind you, stand in front of a mirror. Rotate your arms without moving your elbows away from your body so that your palms face the mirror. If your range of motion is good, your palms should be entirely visible.

The exercises on the pages that follow will help you restore or maintain flexibility in your joints by gently stretching the muscles and connective tissues in your upper body. Perform them in order, then do the exercises for the middle and lower body. Begin slowly with five repetitions for each exercise and work your way up to 10.

WALK-AWAY Stand near a wall with your feet apart, your left hand on your hip and your right palm against the wall a little higher than your shoulder *(far left)*. Walk your hand up the wall as high as you can, straightening your elbow *(center)*. Then move your right foot next to your left *(above)*.

95

WALL PUSH-UP Stand with your feet apart about 18 inches from a wall, then lean against it with your palms about shoulder-width apart at chin level *(above)*. Push yourself away from the wall, straightening your elbows *(right)*.

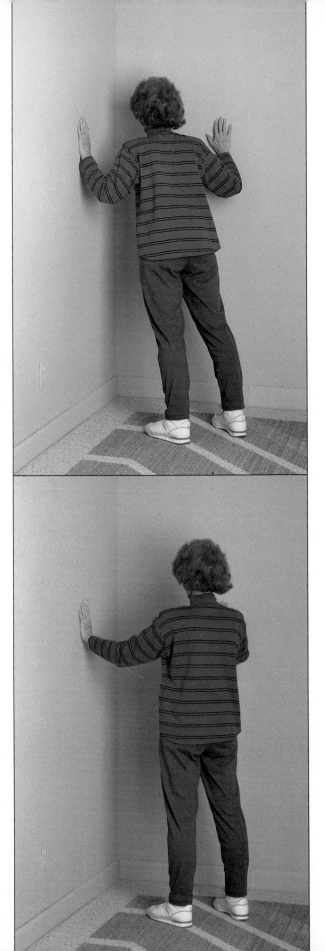

Lean into a corner with your feet spread shoulder-width apart and your palms on the walls a little above shoulder height *(top)*. Push yourself away from the corner *(left)*.

97

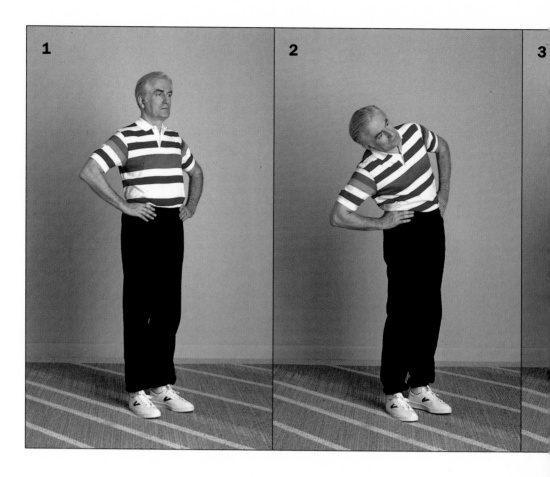

The Upper Body/3

SIDE CIRCLE With your hands on your hips and your feet apart (1), keeping your torso aligned, bend to the right (2), then to the left (3). Bending your knees, lean backward (4), and finally, straightening your knees and keeping your back straight, bend forward until your torso is parallel to the floor (5).

To make the above exercise harder, clasp your hands behind you when you bend forward (1), then backward (2). Extend your arms at shoulder height when you bend to the sides (3,4).

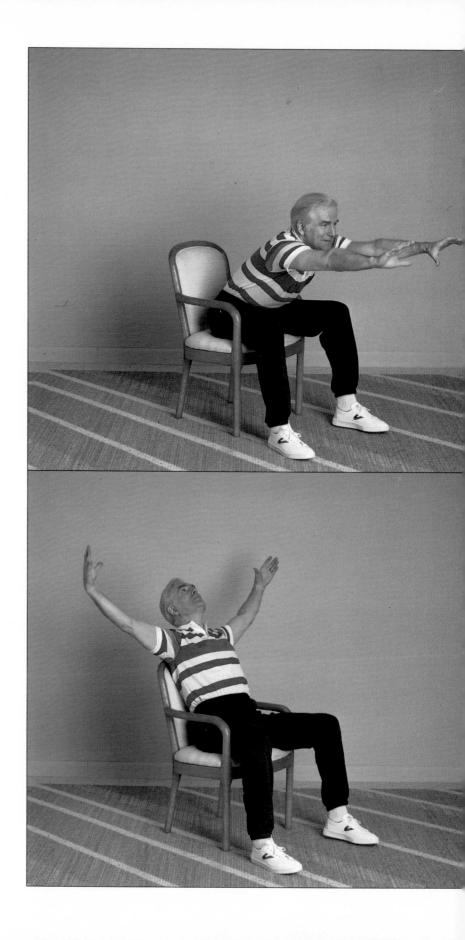

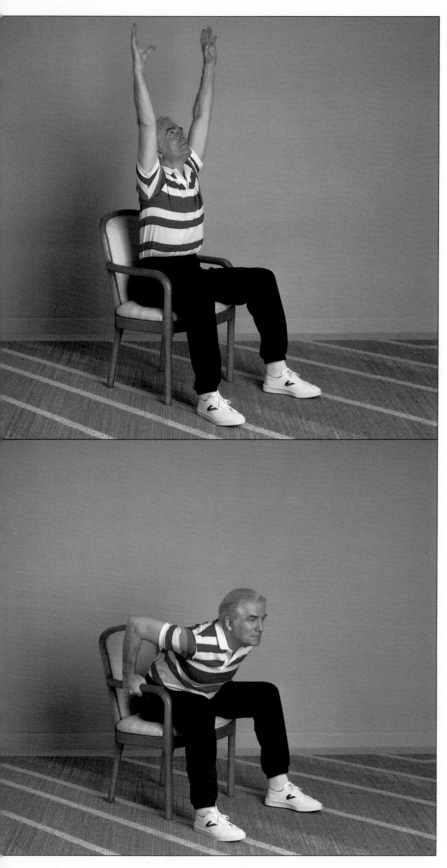

The Upper Body/4

ARM CIRCLE Sit in a chair with your arms and legs spread apart and reach forward, keeping your back straight *(opposite left)*. Sit back until your torso is straight and raise your arms toward the ceiling *(left)*. Then open your arms wide *(opposite below)* as you lean back as far as you can. Grasp the arms of the chair as you lean forward again *(below left)*. Return to the starting position.

The Middle Body/1

To counteract the effects of aging on your posture, you must exercise your abdominal muscles, which support a well-aligned spine. If you do not exercise them, they are apt to weaken and atrophy; in addition to the natural degeneration of bone, the result can be a bowed spine, narrowed shoulders and a pot belly.

If you tone your abs, your stance will be more erect, your lungs more capable of full expansion to get the most oxygen, because your back will be less likely to ache. Perform the entire abdominal routine at least three times per week for maximum benefit. Begin with five repetitions for each exercise and work your way up to 10.

KNEE LIFT Lying on a mat with your arms at your sides and your feet comfortably apart *(below)*, alternately raise each knee toward your chest, then lower it.

LEG RAISE Lying supine with your arms at your sides, bend both knees toward your chest (1). Extend your right leg as you lower your bent left leg (2). Raise both knees toward your chest again (3), then extend your left leg as you lower your bent right knee (4).

PELVIC TILT Lying on a mat with your feet flat and your knees bent, place your hands just under your buttocks *(opposite)*. Use your abdominal muscles to lift your buttocks up and align your body from knees to shoulders *(above)*. Lower yourself to the starting position.

CRUNCH Lie on a mat with your knees bent and your hands clasped behind your head. Contract your abdominals and raise your left shoulder and your right knee to touch your left elbow *(inset opposite)*. Return to the starting position *(inset left)*. Then raise your right shoulder and touch your right elbow to your lifted left knee *(below left)*.

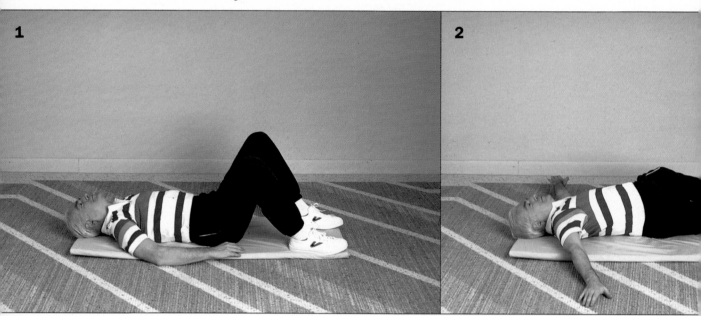

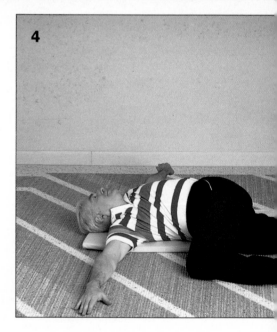

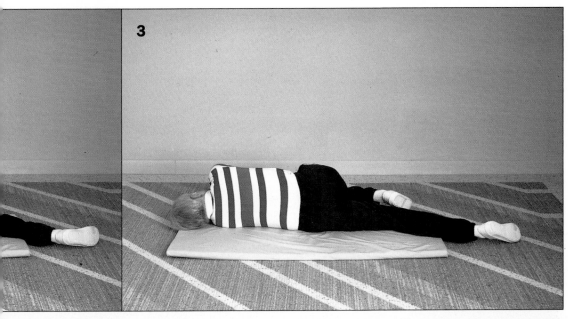

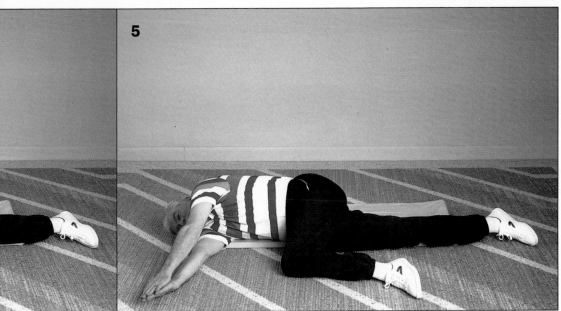

SWING-OVER Lying on your back with your knees bent and your arms at your sides (1), raise your arms to shoulder level as you extend your left leg and swing your bent right leg over it. Try to keep your right arm on the floor (2). Then raise your right arm straight up and over your body and down on top of your extended left arm (3). Lift your right arm again as you straighten your right leg and swing your bent left leg over it, keeping your extended left arm on the floor if possible (4). Finally, bring your left arm over your body to meet your right (5). Return to the starting position.

The Middle Body/5

PELVIC ROCK On your hands and knees with your legs spread comfortably apart, let your midsection droop, but keep your head aligned with your spine *(below)*. Round your back and drop your head as you curl your toes under *(bottom)*. Return to the starting position *(right)*.

LEG CIRCLE On your hands and knees *(above)*, circle your right leg forward and grasp your ankle with your right hand *(above center)*. Return to the starting position. Then circle your right leg to extend straight back, slightly above hip height *(above right)*. Return to the starting position. Circle your left leg forward and grasp your ankle with your left hand *(near right)*. Return to the starting position. Circle your left leg straight behind you *(far right)*. Return to the starting position.

The Lower Body/1

To minimize the risk of falling as you get older, you should keep your lower body muscles toned. Strong muscles not only facilitate balance, they make it possible for you to recover from slightly unstable positions.

Whichever aerobic activity you choose for maintaining your cardiovascular fitness, exercise for your lower body should be included. Jogging, walking and bicycling are all excellent conditioners that strengthen your legs and thighs.

The exercises on the following eight pages will help you maintain muscle tone and flexibility in your lower body even if your cardiovascular exercise is primarily for your upper body, such as rowing. Perform them five times each to begin and work your way up to 10.

Movements like the Number Four on page 116 and the Leg Stretch on page 118 will help you increase the range of motion in your hip joints, for example, making falls less likely. The Twist on page 121 is a stretch for your entire body, so it should be performed at the end of your exercise routine.

The Lower Body/2

SPRINTER'S START On your hands and knees, with your hands slightly more than shoulder-width apart *(above)*, bring your left knee under your chest and extend your right leg so that your thigh forms a 45-degree angle with the mat *(opposite top)*. Curl your right toes under, straighten your right leg and rise up on your left foot as you flex it and straighten your back *(opposite bottom)*.

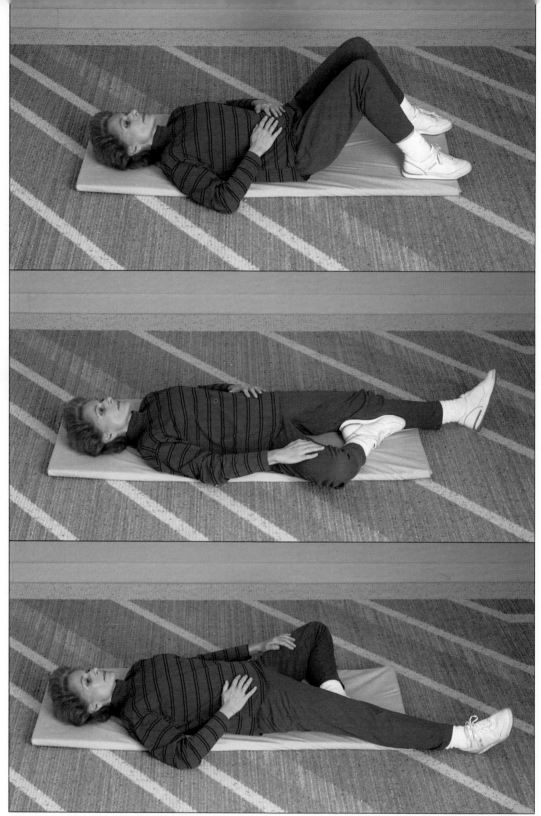

The Lower Body/3

NUMBER FOUR Lying on a mat with your knees bent, place your hands on your lower abdomen *(top)*. Extend your left leg and let your right knee fall to the mat, placing your right foot against your left calf *(center)*. Return to the starting position and repeat for your right leg *(above)*. Alternate legs.

To make this exercise more difficult, extend your arms above your head *(below)*. Alternate legs, following the directions on the opposite page without using your hands.

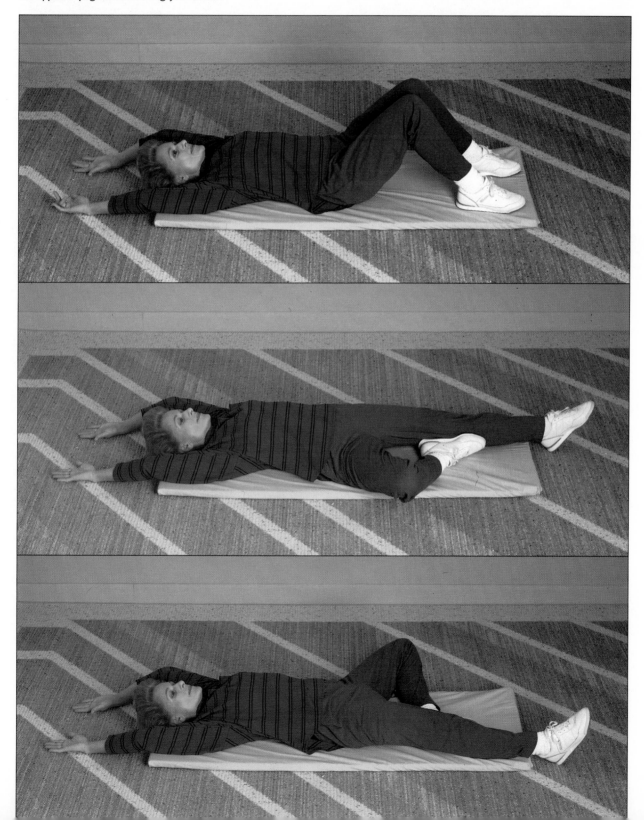

The Lower Body/4

LEG STRETCH Lie on a mat with your hands clasped behind your head and your knees bent *(top)*. Raise your right foot, straighten your knee and flex your foot *(opposite top)*. Keeping your foot flexed, raise your leg higher *(above)*. Then lower your leg as you point your foot *(opposite center)*. Alternate legs.

To make this exercise more difficult, extend your arms behind your head *(left)*.

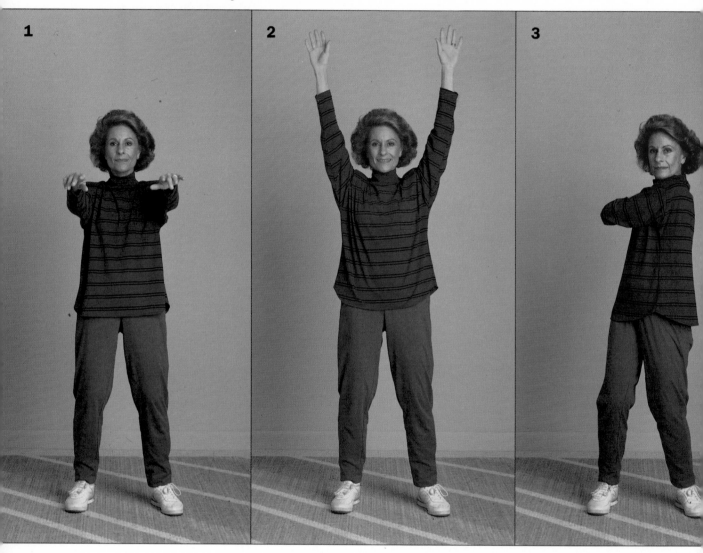

4

5

TWIST Stand with your legs comfortably apart and extend your arms in front of you at shoulder height (1). Raise your arms as high as you can (2), then bring them back to shoulder height in front of you and twist them to your right without turning your head (3). Bring them to the front once again, and swing them to your left (4). Return to the starting position (5).

CHAPTER FOUR

Cholesterol

Minimizing the risks — a lifelong way to eat

Cholesterol is a natural substance manufactured in your body and also found in the food you eat. It is essential to life — and yet too much of it can kill you. In recent years, no element of nutrition has received as much attention as cholesterol. Books about it appear on best-seller lists, and more and more foods are touted as being cholesterol-free. Yet, while many Americans are aware that a high blood cholesterol level is not good for them — that it is directly connected with heart disease, the leading cause of mortality — they nevertheless do not understand which foods, and specifically which fats, raise their cholesterol levels, or why a food like oat bran is beneficial while cream, butter, fried foods, salad dressing and avocados are not. Another common misunderstanding is the difference between "good" and "bad" cholesterol, and how your diet regulates the amount of each in your bloodstream. This chapter clarifies what is known about cholesterol and provides recipes to help you limit the amount of fat in your diet.

123

What is cholesterol?

Cholesterol is a lipid — a soft, waxy white substance made in the body by the liver — that has several functions. It is a building block of cell membranes, a vital component of the protective sheaths surrounding nerve fibers and a constituent of bile, which is necessary to digest fats. Cholesterol is also used in the production of hormones and vitamin D. Because all animals contain this substance— not only in their bloodstreams, but in their tissues — cholesterol is present in all animal products: meat, poultry, fish, eggs and dairy products. However, it is not an essential dietary nutrient, because your body makes all the cholesterol it needs. The type in foods you eat is called dietary cholesterol, but it is identical to the type made in your body.

What is the difference between "good" and "bad" cholesterol?

Technically, there is no such thing as "good" or "bad" cholesterol. These terms refer to how cholesterol is transported through your body. Because it is not soluble either in water or blood, it is wrapped in two types of protein packages called lipoproteins: low-density lipoprotein (LDL) and high-density lipoprotein (HDL). The density is what determines how good or bad the cholesterol is for you.

LDL delivers cholesterol as building material to your cells. But when your cells have used a sufficient amount, LDL deposits the excess cholesterol in the walls of your blood vessels, forming nodules called plaque, which partially obstructs the vessels. This leads to a condition called atherosclerosis that restricts the flow of blood and can eventually cause a heart attack or stroke. For this reason, LDL has been labeled "bad" cholesterol. Studies have shown that the higher the level of LDL, the greater the risk of atherosclerosis.

HDL, in contrast, contains a smaller percentage of cholesterol and a greater amount of protein than LDL does, and it appears to play a role in removing cholesterol from circulation, transporting it back to the liver to be processed or eliminated. Researchers have noted that people with high HDL blood levels have less atherosclerosis and, consequently, less heart disease than people with lower levels of HDL. HDL is therefore referred to as "good" cholesterol. Researchers contend that women have fewer heart attacks than men because they have naturally higher levels of HDL cholesterol.

What determines your cholesterol level?

A number of factors can influence how much of each type of cholesterol you have in your bloodstream: your diet, weight, heredity, the amount of aerobic exercise you perform, whether or not you smoke or use certain oral contraceptives, your personality style and how you cope with stress. Performing aerobic exercise, maintaining your ideal weight and not smoking all contribute to keeping your LDL level low.

Until recently, the influence of dietary fat and cholesterol on the amount of HDL and LDL in the blood was not clear. But now, the

FATS	PERCENTAGE OF FATTY ACIDS			
	Saturated	Monounsaturated	Polyunsaturated	Other
Canola (rapeseed) oil	7	56	33	
Safflower oil	9	12	75	
Walnut oil	9	23	63	
Sunflower oil	10	20	66	
Corn oil	13	24	59	
Olive oil	14	74	8	
Sesame oil	14	40	42	
Soybean oil	14	23	58	
Margarine, soft tub	14	14	50	
Margarine, stick	15	37	25	
Peanut oil	17	46	32	
Cottonseed oil	26	18	52	
Chicken fat (11 mg cholesterol/tb)	30	45	21	
Lard, pork (12 mg cholesterol/tb)	40	45	11	
Palm oil	49	37	9	
Beef tallow (14 mg cholesterol/tb)	50	42		4
Butter (33 mg cholesterol/tb)	62	29		4
Cocoa butter	60	33		3
Palm-kernel oil	81	11		2
Coconut oil	87	6		2

The saturated, monounsaturated and polyunsaturated fatty acids do not add up to 100 percent because other fat compounds are present. Source: U.S. Department of Agriculture Handbook No. 8-4

Saturated fatty acids Monounsaturated fatty acids Polyunsaturated fatty acids Other fat compounds

most extensive report on diet and health ever prepared by the United States government, *The Surgeon General's Report on Nutrition and Health,* has linked a high intake of saturated fats and dietary cholesterol to high blood cholesterol and an increased risk of coronary heart disease.

Although consuming cholesterol in foods does contribute to the level of LDL in your blood, researchers have found that eating saturated fat is actually more influential. LDL is derived mainly from triglycerides, the fat in food and particularly in saturated fat, which is found in butter and dairy products, meats, hard cheeses like Cheddar, and tropical vegetable oils (notably palm, palm kernel oil and coconut). These oils are used in many processed foods: for example, some commercially made muffins, pasta sauces, store-bought cookies and crackers, frozen entrees, canned soups and salad dressings.

What is a safe level of cholesterol in your body?
The average American's cholesterol is 215 milligrams per 100 milliliters of blood — lower than it used to be, but still too high. It should be below 200 milligrams; for people over the age of 20, 150 milligrams or lower is considered ideal. A cholesterol level from 200 to 240 milligrams is considered borderline high; a reading above 240 milligrams indicates a high risk for heart disease. And every 1 percent rise in cholesterol increases the risk of a heart attack by 2 percent.

Should you go on a special diet to lower your cholesterol?
No. If you maximize the amount of complex carbohydrates and fiber you eat — whole grains, legumes, vegetables and fruits — and minimize your intake of saturated fats and cholesterol — meats, hard cheeses, whole-milk dairy products and fried foods — you will be eating the best diet to reduce LDL cholesterol and increase HDL. Scientists recommend that you eat no more than 300 milligrams of cholesterol per day — the amount in one egg yolk. (The average American consumes 450 milligrams of dietary cholesterol per day.)

For most people, 60 percent of the calories in their diet should come from carbohydrates and 30 percent from fats. Only 10 percent of total calories should come from saturated fats: The remaining 20 percent of the fat calories should consist of polyunsaturated fats (such as corn and safflower oils) and monounsaturated fats (such as olive and canola oils). Most Americans consume about 40 percent of their total calories from fat, and 15 to 17 percent from saturated fat.

What are the benefits of eating oat bran?
A particular soluble fiber, which is found in oat bran, may be effective in reducing cholesterol levels in the blood. Like other fiber found in wheat bran, whole wheat and other grains, oat-bran fiber helps digestion, and, in sufficient quantities, has also been shown to lower LDL and raise HDL levels. However, exactly how much soluble fiber is necessary to lower cholesterol is not certain. One study showed that a cup and a half per day — enough cereal, for example, for a family of four, or a bowl of oatmeal and five oat-bran muffins a day — reduced the blood cholesterol levels of research subjects by 13 to 19 percent. However, eating so many muffins would make it difficult to maintain a balanced diet and not consume too many calories. This is particularly true if you eat commercially prepared muffins, which are often high in calories and saturated fat.

What about eating omega-3 fatty acids?
Certain oily fish, such as tuna, salmon, mackerel, herring, sardines and some shellfish, contain omega-3 polyunsaturated fatty acids. These have been shown not only to lower blood cholesterol, but to

diminish blood clotting, which reduces the chance of heart attack. Although moderately high in cholesterol, oily fish are low in saturated fat, and since their omega-3 fatty acids reduce total blood cholesterol levels, they are a valuable addition to a healthy diet. (For recipes that use these and other fish, see pages 132, 136 and 137.) And because shrimp, lobster and squid are also rich sources of omega-3, they are considered to be good alternatives to red meats. Taking fish-oil supplements is not recommended, since an optimal dose has not yet been determined for this nutrient.

Will olive and canola oils also help reduce cholesterol?

Possibly. Both these oils are monounsaturated, and some clinical studies have suggested that they not only help lower your total blood cholesterol levels, but also maintain or increase your HDL level. Taking monounsaturated oil as a supplement is not advisable, since Americans already have too much fat in their diets. Use these oils instead of butter, which is highly saturated, when you cook.

Can cholesterol-lowering medication help?

Fortunately, several studies have shown that adjusting your diet is actually more successful and a lot less expensive for lowering serum cholesterol levels than taking the new drug Lovastatin and the B vitamin, niacin. Drugs have side effects; at best, your doctor would prescribe them along with a healthy diet, since no amount of medication can reverse the bad effects of eating large amounts of saturated fats and cholesterol.

Should children's diets be low in fat and cholesterol?

The question of whether children should follow the same low-fat, low-cholesterol diet that is recommended for adults is still quite controversial. However, the American Heart Association and a panel of experts convened by the National Institutes of Health recommend that children over age two should limit their fat and cholesterol intake to 30 percent of their total calories, with less than 10 percent of the calories coming from saturated fat. They believe that limiting fat and cholesterol intake early in life will help to prevent the buildup of fatty deposits that may result in heart attacks and strokes.

Researchers have found that some children start to develop the fatty deposits of atherosclerosis very early in life. These deposits have been discovered in the coronary arteries of young people around the age of puberty. Studies have shown that there are fatty streaks in the aortas of some children between eight and 10 years of age. Many health authorities also believe that since eating habits are formed at an early age, a low-fat, low-cholesterol diet can help a child develop eating habits that will reduce the risk of heart disease later in life.

The recipes that follow are especially low in saturated fats and cholesterol and high in complex carbohydrates and fiber, a regimen that is necessary for a healthy diet.

Blueberry-Oat-Bran Muffins, Raspberry-Tangerine Juice

Breakfast
·····················

BLUEBERRY-OAT-BRAN MUFFINS

You can substitute oat bran, an excellent source of cholesterol-lowering soluble fiber, for up to one third of the flour in most muffin recipes.

CALORIES per muffin	135
64% Carbohydrate	22 g
13% Protein	4 g
23% Fat	4 g
CALCIUM	71 mg
IRON	1 mg
SODIUM	114 mg

1 1/2 cups fresh or unsweetened
   frozen blueberries
1 cup buttermilk
1/4 cup honey
2 tablespoons sunflower oil
2 egg whites, lightly beaten

1 cup rolled oats
1 cup oat bran
1/2 cup unbleached
   all-purpose flour
2 teaspoons baking powder
Pinch of salt

Preheat the oven to 375° F. Line 12 muffin tin cups with paper liners; set aside. If using fresh blueberries, wash and pick them over. In a small bowl stir together the buttermilk, honey, oil and egg whites. In a large bowl stir together the oats, oat bran, flour, baking powder and salt, and make a well in the center. Pour in the milk mixture and the blueberries, and stir just until combined; do not overmix. Divide the batter among the muffin tin cups and bake for 25 minutes, or until a toothpick inserted into the center of a muffin comes out clean and dry.

Makes 12 muffins

RASPBERRY-TANGERINE JUICE

Uncooked raspberries are a good source of soluble fiber. They also supply insoluble fiber, which may help prevent colon cancer.

CALORIES per serving	138
90% Carbohydrate	32 g
5% Protein	2 g
5% Fat	1 g
CALCIUM	62 mg
IRON	1 mg
SODIUM	3 mg

2 cups raspberries

1/2 cup chopped fresh mint, plus
  4 mint sprigs for garnish

1 quart fresh or reconstituted
  frozen tangerine juice

Crushed ice

If using fresh raspberries, wash and pat them dry. Place the raspberries and chopped mint in a food processor or blender and process for 1 minute, or until puréed. Stir in the tangerine juice. To serve, fill 4 tall glasses with crushed ice, pour the juice over it and garnish with mint sprigs. Makes 4 servings

PEAR AND DRIED FRUIT CRISP

Polyunsaturated fats, such as safflower oil, help lower total blood cholesterol and should be used instead of butter whenever possible.

4 medium-size ripe pears (about
  1 1/2 pounds total weight)

1/2 pound mixed dried fruit

5 tablespoons brown sugar

2 tablespoons lemon juice

1 1/2 teaspoons ground cinnamon

2 slices stale whole-wheat
  bread, cut into 1/2-inch cubes

1 cup rolled oats

1/4 cup unbleached
  all-purpose flour

3 tablespoons safflower oil

CALORIES per serving	261
74% Carbohydrate	51 g
5% Protein	4 g
21% Fat	6 g
CALCIUM	44 mg
IRON	2 mg
SODIUM	39 mg

Preheat the oven to 375° F. Meanwhile, halve, stem and core but do not peel the pears. Cut them into 3/4-inch-thick slices and place them in an 11 x 7-inch baking dish. Cut the dried fruit into 3/4-inch pieces and add it to the pears. Add 2 tablespoons of sugar, the lemon juice and 3/4 teaspoon of cinnamon, and toss gently. Stir in the bread and set aside.

For the topping, in a small bowl stir together the oats, flour, and the remaining sugar and cinnamon. Add the oil and stir until the mixture is crumbly. Spread the topping over the pear mixture and bake for 20 minutes, or until the dried fruit is soft and the topping is crisp. Makes 8 servings

BANANA-APPLE SMOOTHIE

The fiber in the banana, applesauce and oat bran not only lowers your cholesterol, but also helps keep your stomach feeling full longer.

1 ripe banana

1/2 cup plain lowfat yogurt

1/2 cup unsweetened applesauce

1/4 cup skim milk

1 tablespoon honey

2 tablespoons oat bran

CALORIES per serving	178
80% Carbohydrate	37 g
12% Protein	6 g
8% Fat	2 g
CALCIUM	152 mg
IRON	1 mg
SODIUM	58 mg

Peel the banana and cut it into large chunks. Place the banana, yogurt, applesauce, milk and honey in a food processor or blender, and process for 1 to 2 minutes, or until smooth. Add the oat bran and process for another 5 to 10 seconds, or until thickened. Divide the smoothie between 2 tall glasses and serve immediately. Makes 2 servings

FRESH FRUIT WITH ORANGE YOGURT SAUCE

CALORIES per serving	276
84% Carbohydrate	62 g
9% Protein	7 g
7% Fat	2 g
CALCIUM	178 mg
IRON	1 mg
SODIUM	59 mg

When you eat fresh fruits instead of drinking juices, you consume much more fiber. Citrus fruits are particularly rich sources of soluble fiber.

1/3 cup plain lowfat yogurt
1 tablespoon frozen orange
  juice concentrate
2 teaspoons brown sugar

1 banana
1/4 cup fresh blueberries
1/2 cup pink grapefruit sections
1 teaspoon oat bran

In a small bowl stir together the yogurt, orange juice concentrate and sugar; set aside. Peel and slice the banana. Wash and pick over the blueberries. Combine the banana, berries and grapefruit in a small bowl, pour the sauce on top, sprinkle with the oat bran and serve immediately.   Makes 1 serving

CURRANT-CORN MUFFINS

CALORIES per muffin	137
70% Carbohydrate	24 g
11% Protein	4 g
19% Fat	3 g
CALCIUM	89 mg
IRON	1 mg
SODIUM	157 mg

Choose a margarine made with polyunsaturated oil, and look for one that lists liquid (not hydrogenated) vegetable oil as the first ingredient.

1 egg white, lightly beaten
1 cup skim milk
2 tablespoons margarine, melted
  and cooled
1/2 cup unbleached
  all-purpose flour

1 1/4 cups cornmeal
1/2 cup dried currants
1/4 cup wheat germ
2 teaspoons baking powder
1 tablespoon sugar
Pinch of salt

Preheat the oven to 425° F. Line 12 muffin tin cups with paper liners; set aside. In a small bowl stir together the egg white, milk and margarine; set aside. In a large bowl stir together the flour, cornmeal, currants, wheat germ, baking powder, sugar and salt, and make a well in the center. Pour the egg mixture into the well and stir just until combined. Divide the batter among the muffin tin cups and bake for 20 to 25 minutes, or until a toothpick inserted into the center of a muffin comes out clean and dry.   Makes 12 muffins

STRAWBERRY-ORANGE SHAKE

CALORIES per serving	342
82% Carbohydrate	73 g
10% Protein	9 g
8% Fat	3 g
CALCIUM	206 mg
IRON	2 mg
SODIUM	134 mg

Oat bran and buttermilk make this beverage thick and creamy, but it contains only three grams of fat and five milligrams of cholesterol.

1 1/2 cups fresh or unsweetened
  frozen strawberries
1/2 cup buttermilk
1/4 cup frozen orange
  juice concentrate

1 tablespoon honey
1/4 teaspoon orange extract
2 tablespoons oat bran

If using fresh strawberries, wash and hull them. Place the berries in a food processor or blender, add the buttermilk, orange juice concentrate, honey and orange extract, and process for 1 to 2 minutes, or until smooth. Add the oat bran and process for another 5 to 10 seconds, or until thickened. Pour the shake into a tall glass and serve immediately.   Makes 1 serving

Lunch

CARROT-BEET SOUP

Soups thickened with puréed vegetables, like this combination of carrots and beets, need no high-cholesterol butter or cream to enrich them.

1 tablespoon corn oil
1 cup coarsely chopped onion
1/2 cup chopped shallots
2 cups peeled, sliced fresh beets

2 cup sliced carrots
3 cups low-sodium chicken stock
4 thin lemon slices for garnish

CALORIES per serving	141
58% Carbohydrate	21 g
12% Protein	4 g
30% Fat	5 g
CALCIUM	47 mg
IRON	2 mg
SODIUM	117 mg

Heat the oil in a medium-size saucepan over medium heat. Add the onion and shallots, and cook, stirring frequently, for 10 minutes. Add the beets, carrots and stock, increase the heat to medium-high and bring the mixture to a boil. Cover the pan, reduce the the heat to medium low and simmer for 30 minutes, or until the vegetables are tender. Remove the pan from the heat and allow the soup to cool slightly, then transfer the solids to a food processor and process for 1 minute, or until puréed. Return the purée to the soup. Let the soup cool, then cover and refrigerate it until well chilled. Stir the soup, ladle it into 4 bowls and garnish with lemon slices.   Makes 4 servings

Carrot-Beet Soup

TEXAS CAVIAR

Research reported in The American Journal of Clinical Nutrition indicates that eating garlic increases blood levels of high-density lipoproteins, the "good" cholesterol. Several studies have shown raw onions to have the same effect.

One 10-ounce package frozen black-eyed peas	1 garlic clove, peeled and crushed
1/3 cup red wine vinegar	1/4 teaspoon salt
1 tablespoon plus 2 teaspoons sunflower oil	1/4 teaspoon ground pepper
2 tablespoons chopped fresh parsley	6 ounces cherry tomatoes
	1 cup coarsely chopped onion
	1/4 pound green beans

The day before serving, place the peas and 1 cup of water in a medium-size saucepan and bring to a boil over high heat, separating the peas with a fork. Cover the pan, reduce the heat to medium and cook for 10 minutes. Meanwhile, for the dressing, in a large bowl whisk together the vinegar, oil, parsley, garlic, salt and pepper; set aside.

Wash, stem and halve the tomatoes; set aside. When the peas are cooked, drain them thoroughly, let them cool slightly and then add them to the bowl of dressing. Add the tomatoes and onion, and stir to combine. Cover the bowl and refrigerate the salad overnight.

At least 1 hour before serving, bring a small saucepan of water to a boil. Meanwhile, wash and trim the green beans, and cut them into 1-inch lengths. Blanch the beans for 5 minutes, or until crisp-tender, then drain, cool under cold running water and drain again. Add the beans to the salad and toss gently. Let the salad stand at room temperature until ready to serve. Makes 4 servings

CALORIES per serving	183
54% Carbohydrate	25 g
16% Protein	8 g
30% Fat	6 g
CALCIUM	49 mg
IRON	2 mg
SODIUM	147 mg

OYSTER-POTATO HASH

Omega-3, the cholesterol-lowering polyunsaturated fat found in oysters and other seafood, also reduces the level of blood triglycerides.

1 1/2 pounds potatoes, boiled and cooled	1/4 teaspoon salt
2 tablespoons safflower oil	1/4 teaspoon ground pepper
1 cup coarsely chopped red onion	2 ounces raw oysters (4 to 5 medium-size oysters)
2 garlic cloves, chopped	1/2 cup chopped fresh cilantro or parsley
1 cup diced red bell pepper	
1 cup diced carrots	

Quarter the unpeeled potatoes, then cut the quarters into 1/4-inch-thick slices and set aside. Heat the oil in a large nonstick skillet over medium heat, add the onion and garlic, and sauté for 10 minutes, or until softened. Add the potatoes, bell pepper, carrots, salt and pepper, cover the pan and cook for 15 minutes, or until the carrots are crisp-tender. Meanwhile, coarsely chop the oysters. Stir the oysters and cilantro into the hash, and cook, stirring occasionally, for 5 minutes, or until the oysters are firm. Divide the hash among 4 plates and serve. Makes 4 servings

CALORIES per serving	234
62% Carbohydrate	37 g
10% Protein	6 g
28% Fat	8 g
CALCIUM	55 mg
IRON	4 mg
SODIUM	178 mg

CREAMY SALSA WITH DIPPERS

Lowfat yogurt is a healthy base for dips and dressings: It contains about one sixth the cholesterol and less than one twelfth the saturated fat of dairy sour cream.

1 pound plum tomatoes
1 medium-size onion
1 jalapeño pepper
1/4 cup plain lowfat yogurt
1/4 cup chopped fresh cilantro
1/2 teaspoon salt
1/4 teaspoon ground pepper

1 1/2 pounds new potatoes
2 cups cauliflower florets
1 1/3 cups broccoli florets
1/4 pound green beans
1 red bell pepper
4 large flour tortillas

CALORIES per serving	312
78% Carbohydrate	64 g
14% Protein	11 g
8% Fat	3 g
CALCIUM	134 mg
IRON	4 mg
SODIUM	326 mg

For the salsa, core and dice the tomatoes. Peel and coarsely chop the onion. Seed and chop the jalapeño. In a food processor or blender, working in batches if necessary, combine the tomatoes, onion, jalapeño, yogurt, cilantro, salt and pepper. Process the mixture, pulsing the machine on and off, until the vegetables are coarsely chopped. Transfer the salsa to a bowl and set aside.

Preheat the oven to 500° F. Bring 2 medium-size saucepans of water to a boil. Cook the potatoes in one pan for 20 minutes, or until tender. Meanwhile, blanch the cauliflower in the other pan for 3 minutes, or until crisp-tender. Reserving the boiling water, transfer the cauliflower to a colander, cool it under cold running water and set aside to drain. Blanch, cool and drain the broccoli and beans in the same fashion. Stem and core the bell pepper, and cut it into wide strips; set aside. Dip each tortilla in a bowl of water, then cut it into 8 triangles. Place them on a baking sheet and bake for 3 to 4 minutes, or until crisp. Reduce the oven temperature to 300° F and bake them for another 2 to 3 minutes, or until just beginning to brown. Remove them from the oven and set aside. Drain the potatoes and cut them into thick slices.

To serve, place the bowl of salsa in the center of a platter and surround it with the vegetables and tortilla chips.   Makes 4 servings

TOFU-CARROT SANDWICHES

Monounsaturated fats, found in olive oil, can lower the levels of dangerous LDL cholesterol without reducing the healthy HDL, which carries cholesterol out of the bloodstream.

CALORIES per serving	299
54% Carbohydrate	40 g
19% Protein	14 g
27% Fat	9 g
CALCIUM	191 mg
IRON	7 mg
SODIUM	377 mg

3 cups sliced carrots
6 ounces firm tofu, well drained
1 tablespoon olive oil
2 teaspoons Dijon-style mustard
1 garlic clove, peeled

1/4 teaspoon salt
1/4 teaspoon ground pepper
8 slices whole-wheat bread
8 large Romaine lettuce leaves
2 cups alfalfa sprouts

Bring a medium-size saucepan of water to a boil. Add the carrots and cook for about 15 minutes, or until tender; drain and set aside to cool. Combine the carrots, tofu, oil, mustard, garlic, salt and pepper in a food processor or blender, and process until smooth; set aside. Toast the bread. Place a folded lettuce leaf on each slice of toast and top it with the carrot spread and sprouts. Cut the open-face sandwiches in half and serve.   Makes 4 servings

Dinner

BLACK BEAN SALAD

Legumes—dried beans and peas—are excellent sources of guar gum and pectin, types of soluble fiber that can lower blood cholesterol levels.

CALORIES per serving	250
54% Carbohydrate	35 g
15% Protein	10 g
31% Fat	9 g
CALCIUM	76 mg
IRON	3 mg
SODIUM	323 mg

1/3 cup white wine vinegar
2 tablespoons corn oil
1 tablespoon Dijon-style mustard
1 teaspoon Oriental sesame oil
1 garlic clove, peeled and minced
1 teaspoon dried tarragon
1/4 teaspoon salt
1/4 teaspoon ground pepper

2 cups canned black beans, rinsed and drained
1 cup diced celery
1 red bell pepper, thinly sliced
6 ounces small fresh beets, trimmed
2 cups sliced carrots
2 cups shredded Romaine lettuce

In a large bowl whisk together the vinegar, corn oil, mustard, sesame oil, garlic, tarragon, salt and ground pepper. Add the beans, celery and bell pepper, and toss well; set aside at room temperature.

Bring 2 cups of water to a boil in a medium-size saucepan over medium-high heat. Add the beets, cover the pan, reduce the heat to medium-low and simmer for 15 minutes, or until the beets are tender when pierced with a sharp knife. Add the carrots and cook for 5 minutes, or until crisp-tender. Drain the beets and carrots, cool under cold running water and set aside to drain.

Black Bean Salad

Halve the beets and cut them into 1/4-inch-thick slices. Add the beets, carrots and Romaine to the salad and toss to combine. Let the salad stand at room temperature for at least 1 hour before serving.   Makes 4 servings

CAPELLINI WITH ARTICHOKES

Substituting high-protein, lowfat foods like pasta and chickpeas for some of the meat in your diet can contribute substantially to lowering your cholesterol.

1/2 pound mushrooms	1 1/2 cups frozen artichoke hearts,
1 red onion, peeled	thawed and drained
2 garlic cloves, peeled	1 teaspoon dried oregano
1 cup low-sodium chicken stock	Pinch of salt
1/2 cup canned chickpeas,	1/2 pound capellini or spaghetti
rinsed and drained	1/4 cup chopped fresh parsley
3 tablespoons olive oil	1/4 teaspoon ground pepper

Wash, trim and coarsely chop the mushrooms; coarsely chop the onion and garlic. Place the stock and chickpeas in a medium-size saucepan and bring to a boil over medium-high heat. Cover the pan, reduce the heat to medium-low and simmer for 15 minutes. Meanwhile, heat 2 tablespoons of oil in a large skillet over medium-high heat. Add the onion and garlic, and cook, stirring occasionally, for 10 minutes, or until softened; set aside. Reserving the stock, transfer the chickpeas to a food processor or blender and process until puréed; set aside.

Bring a large pot of water to a boil. Cook the capellini for 8 minutes, or according to the package directions, until al dente. Meanwhile, return the stock to a boil. Add the mushrooms, artichokes, oregano and salt, and simmer, stirring occasionally, for 5 minutes. Drain the pasta and toss it with the remaining oil. Add the chickpea purée, the stock, vegetables, parsley and pepper, toss again and serve immediately.   Makes 4 servings

CALORIES per serving	395
60% Carbohydrate	61 g
13% Protein	13 g
27% Fat	12 g
CALCIUM	61 mg
IRON	4 mg
SODIUM	172 mg

MIXED BEAN CHILI

If you are eating less meat to cut down on saturated fat, adding beans and other legumes to your diet will help ensure sufficient iron intake.

2 tablespoons safflower oil	One 28-ounce can crushed
1 cup coarsely chopped onion	tomatoes
3 garlic cloves, chopped	1/4 cup mild blended chili powder
2 cups each canned kidney	1/2 teaspoon paprika
beans, pinto beans and	1/4 teaspoon salt
chickpeas, rinsed and drained	

Heat the oil in a large saucepan over medium heat, add the onion and garlic, and sauté for 10 minutes, or until softened. Add the beans and chickpeas, the tomatoes and their liquid, and stir until combined. Stir in the chili powder, paprika and salt. When the chili comes to a boil, cover the pan, reduce the heat to medium-low and simmer for 30 minutes, or until the flavors are blended. Ladle the chili into 6 bowls and serve.   Makes 6 servings

CALORIES per serving	321
64% Carbohydrate	53 g
17% Protein	14 g
19% Fat	7 g
CALCIUM	137 mg
IRON	5 mg
SODIUM	198 mg

BROWN RICE VEGETABLE PILAF

A study at the USDA showed that calcium pectate, the fiber in the cell walls of carrots, may help lower blood cholesterol.

2 tablespoons sunflower oil
1 cup coarsely chopped onion
1 garlic clove, peeled and chopped
1/2 pound cherry tomatoes
2 cups sliced carrots
1 cup canned kidney beans, rinsed and drained
1 large yellow or red bell pepper, sliced 1/2 inch thick
1 teaspoon dried oregano
1/2 teaspoon salt
1/4 teaspoon ground pepper
3 cups cooked brown rice (1 cup raw)
2 tablespoons chopped fresh parsley
1 tablespoon red wine vinegar

CALORIES per serving	348
68% Carbohydrate	61 g
11% Protein	9 g
21% Fat	8 g
CALCIUM	74 mg
IRON	3 mg
SODIUM	310 mg

Heat the oil in a large nonstick skillet over medium heat, add the onion and garlic, and sauté for 10 minutes, or until softened. Add the tomatoes, carrots, beans, bell pepper, oregano, salt and pepper, and stir to combine. Cover the pan and cook for 15 minutes, or until the carrots are crisp-tender and the tomatoes are softened. Stir in the rice, and cook, stirring occasionally, for 5 minutes more, or until the rice is heated through. Stir in the parsley and vinegar, divide the pilaf among 4 plates and serve. Makes 4 servings

CREAMY TUNA MAC

Water-packed tuna is a lowfat source of omega-3 fatty acids. White tuna contains nearly twice as much of this cholesterol-lowering substance as light tuna.

1/4 cup unbleached all-purpose flour
3 tablespoons plus 1 teaspoon margarine
1 cup low-sodium chicken stock
10 garlic cloves
2 cups broccoli florets
1 cup sliced zucchini
1 1/2 cups chopped scallions
1/2 pound elbow macaroni
1/3 cup water-packed tuna
1/4 teaspoon ground pepper

CALORIES per serving	397
58% Carbohydrate	58 g
17% Protein	17 g
25% Fat	11 g
CALCIUM	91 mg
IRON	4 mg
SODIUM	204 mg

Knead together the flour and margarine until smooth; set aside. Place the stock, 1 cup of water and the garlic in a medium-size saucepan, and bring to a boil over medium-high heat. Cover the pan, reduce the heat to medium-low and simmer for 15 minutes. Using a slotted spoon, remove the garlic; set aside. Add the broccoli and zucchini to the pan, cover and simmer for 5 minutes, or until crisp-tender. Stir in the scallions. Using a slotted spoon, transfer the vegetables to a large serving bowl; set aside. Reserve the liquid.

Bring a large pot of water to a boil. Cook the macaroni for 10 minutes, or according to the package directions, until al dente. Meanwhile, for the sauce, peel the garlic. Place the garlic in a blender and process until puréed; set aside. Bring the cooking liquid to a boil over medium-high heat. Whisk in small pieces of the flour mixture until the sauce is smooth and thick, then stir in the garlic purée.

Drain the macaroni. Add the tuna, macaroni, sauce and pepper to the vegetables, and stir well. Serve immediately. Makes 4 servings

FISH STEW WITH PEPPERS

This dish is much lower in fat than beef stew. Even lean beef like top round contains about five times as much saturated fat as whitefish.

1 1/2 pounds boiling potatoes
1 medium-size green bell pepper
1 medium-size red onion
1 garlic clove
One 14-ounce can plum tomatoes
1 bay leaf

1 teaspoon dried dill
3/4 teaspoon sugar
1/4 pound whitefish filet, cut into
  1-inch pieces
1/4 teaspoon ground pepper
Pinch of salt

CALORIES per serving	204
70% Carbohydrate	37 g
20% Protein	11 g
10% Fat	2 g
CALCIUM	65 mg
IRON	4 mg
SODIUM	223 mg

Wash the potatoes and bell pepper; peel the onion and garlic. Slice the potatoes, pepper and onion 1/4 inch thick, and mince the garlic; set aside. Combine the tomatoes and their liquid, the onions, garlic and bay leaf in a 9-inch nonstick skillet, and bring to a boil over medium-high heat, stirring to break up the tomatoes. Add the potatoes, dill and sugar, and stir to combine. Cover the pan, reduce the heat to medium and simmer, turning the potatoes occasionally, for 15 minutes, or until the potatoes are just tender. Add the bell pepper, cover and cook for 5 minutes more. Add the fish, ground pepper and salt, cover and cook for 2 to 3 minutes, or until the fish is opaque. Remove the bay leaf, divide the stew among 4 bowls and serve.   Makes 4 servings

CAJUN RICE WITH SALMON

This dish offers the health benefits of salmon, a rich dietary source of omega-3 fatty acids, and okra, a good source of soluble fiber.

2 tablespoons corn oil
1 cup coarsely chopped shallots
2 garlic cloves, peeled
  and chopped
1 cup white rice
One 14-ounce can plum tomatoes
One 10-ounce package frozen
  sliced okra (2 cups)
1 cup coarsely chopped celery
1 cup chopped red bell pepper
1 tablespoon tomato paste

1/2 jalapeño pepper, seeded and
  finely chopped
1 teaspoon chili powder
1/2 teaspoon dried thyme
1/4 teaspoon salt
1/4 teaspoon ground pepper
Pinch of cayenne pepper
1/4 pound fresh salmon filet,
  cut into 1/4-inch pieces
Hot pepper sauce to taste

Heat 1 tablespoon of oil in a large nonstick skillet over medium heat, add the shallots and garlic, and sauté for 10 minutes, or until translucent. Add the remaining oil and the rice, and sauté for 5 to 10 minutes more, or until the rice begins to color. Stir in the tomatoes and their liquid, the okra, celery, bell pepper, tomato paste, jalapeño, chili powder, thyme, salt, pepper and cayenne. Add 1 1/2 cups of water and bring to a boil. Cover the pan, reduce the heat to medium-low and simmer, stirring occasionally, for 25 minutes, or until the rice is tender. Add a few tablespoons more water if necessary.

Stir the salmon into the rice, cover the pan and cook for 5 minutes, or until the fish is firm. Season the mixture with hot pepper sauce and serve.

Makes 4 servings

CALORIES per serving	359
63% Carbohydrate	57 g
14% Protein	13 g
23% Fat	10 g
CALCIUM	136 mg
IRON	4 mg
SODIUM	385 mg

Lemon-Lime Sorbet

Desserts

LEMON-LIME SORBET

Skim milk forms the base of this dessert, which derives one percent of its calories from fat and has just two milligrams of cholesterol per serving. Premium ice cream may derive up to 56 percent of its calories from fat; a half cup may contain up to 50 milligrams of cholesterol.

CALORIES per serving	104
83% Carbohydrate	23 g
16% Protein	4 g
1% Fat	.2 g
CALCIUM	150 mg
IRON	.1 mg
SODIUM	63 mg

2 large lemons
1 lime
1/3 cup nonfat dry milk

1 cup skim milk
1/4 cup sugar

Wash the lemons and lime and grate enough peel to measure 1 teaspoon each of lemon and lime peel. Halve and squeeze the fruit. You should have about 2/3 cup lemon juice and 3 tablespoons lime juice; set aside. Place the nonfat dry milk in a medium-size bowl and add the lemon and lime juices and peel. Whisk in the skim milk and sugar, and continue whisking until smooth. Pour the mixture into an ice-cube tray (leave in the dividers to help the mixture freeze more quickly). Freeze the sorbet for 3 hours, or until slushy. Transfer the sorbet to a food processor and process it, pulsing the machine on and off, for about 15 seconds, or until spoonable. Divide the sorbet among 4 dessert dishes and serve.

Makes 4 servings

PUMPKIN PIE

The usual cholesterol-laden whole milk, egg yolks and whipped cream topping are omitted from this pie; high-fiber oat bran is added.

CALORIES per serving	174
68% Carbohydrate	30 g
7% Protein	3 g
25% Fat	5 g
CALCIUM	32 mg
IRON	1 mg
SODIUM	85 mg

1 cup unbleached
  all-purpose flour, approximately
2 tablespoons granulated sugar
Pinch of salt
1/4 cup margarine, well chilled
One 16-ounce can pumpkin purée
1/4 cup oat bran

1/4 cup brown sugar
1/4 cup honey
1/4 cup skim milk
2 egg whites, lightly beaten
2 teaspoons cornstarch
1 teaspoon ground allspice

In a medium-size bowl stir together 1 cup of flour, the granulated sugar and salt. Using a pastry blender or 2 knives, cut in the margarine until the mixture resembles cornmeal. Add 2 to 3 tablespoons of cold water and stir until the dough forms a mass. Knead the dough for 1 minute, then form it into a ball, flatten it into a disk and wrap in plastic wrap. Refrigerate for 20 minutes.

Preheat the oven to 425° F. Lightly flour the work surface and rolling pin. Roll out the dough to a 12-inch disk and carefully transfer it to a 9-inch pie pan. Press the dough into the pan, then trim and flute the edges; set aside.

For the filling, in a medium-size bowl combine the pumpkin purée, oat bran, brown sugar, honey, milk, egg whites, cornstarch and allspice, and stir until well blended. Pour the filling into the crust and bake the pie for 15 minutes. Reduce the heat to 350° F and bake for 30 minutes more, or until the crust is golden and the filling is set. Let the pie cool on a rack for 10 minutes and serve it warm or at room temperature. Makes 10 servings

PINEAPPLE-BERRY FREEZE

One serving of this nearly fat-free dessert contains more than three grams of dietary fiber and supplies almost the full recommended daily amount of vitamin C.

1 large ripe pineapple
  (about 3 1/2 pounds)
2 cups fresh or unsweetened
  frozen strawberries

1/4 cup honey
2 tablespoons lemon juice

CALORIES per serving	127
92% Carbohydrate	33 g
3% Protein	1 g
5% Fat	1 g
CALCIUM	18 mg
IRON	1 mg
SODIUM	4 mg

Using a large knife, trim the leaves from the pineapple, then quarter it lengthwise. Run the knife down the center of each quarter to remove the core, then along the inside of the rind to remove the flesh. Cut out any tough "eyes". Coarsely chop the pineapple: You should have about 8 cups. If using fresh strawberries, wash and hull them; place the berries, pineapple, honey and lemon juice in a food processor, and process the mixture for 1 to 2 minutes, or until coarsely puréed. Transfer the purée to the container of an ice-cream maker and freeze it according to the manufacturer's instructions until just firm. Or follow the directions for freezing the Lemon-Lime Sorbet on page 138.

If not serving the freeze immediately, cover the container tightly and place it in the freezer. If necessary, let the freeze soften at room temperature for 5 minutes, or until soft enough to scoop, before serving. Divide the pineapple-berry freeze among 4 dessert dishes and serve. Makes 6 servings

White Grape Juice Sangria

Snacks and Beverages

WHITE GRAPE JUICE SANGRIA

Whole fruit, with all its healthful fiber, is included in this punch.

2 cups fresh strawberries	2 limes
1 orange	1 1/2 quarts white grape juice
1 apple	Crushed ice

Wash all the fruit. Hull and halve the strawberries. Cut the unpeeled orange into 1/2-inch-thick slices; cut the unpeeled apple and limes into 1/4-inch-thick slices. Place the fruit in a pitcher, pour in the grape juice and stir. Refrigerate the sangria for at least 2 hours. To serve, pour the sangria into 10 ice-filled glasses and divide the fruit among them. Makes 10 servings

CALORIES per serving	124
97% Carbohydrate	32 g
2% Protein	1 g
1% Fat	.2 g
CALCIUM	37 mg
IRON	1 mg
SODIUM	1 mg

BANANA SNACK SQUARES

You can make cakes that are practically cholesterol-free if you bake with egg whites, skim milk and oil and instead of whole eggs, whole milk and butter.

CALORIES per serving	246
65% Carbohydrate	41 g
7% Protein	5 g
28% Fat	8 g
CALCIUM	98 mg
IRON	2 mg
SODIUM	200 mg

Vegetable cooking spray
3 bananas
1 tablespoon lemon juice
1/3 cup dark raisins
1 cup unbleached all-purpose flour
1/2 cup oat bran
6 tablespoons brown sugar

2 teaspoons baking powder
1 teaspoon ground cinnamon
1/4 teaspoon salt
1/2 cup skim milk
1/4 cup vegetable oil
2 egg whites, lightly beaten

Preheat the oven to 350° F. Spray an 8-inch square baking pan with cooking spray; set aside. Peel the bananas, slice them 1/4 inch thick and place them in a medium-size bowl with the lemon juice; mash them slightly with a fork or potato masher, then stir in the raisins and set aside. In a large bowl stir together the flour, oat bran, sugar, baking powder, cinnamon and salt, and make a well in the center; set aside. In a small bowl beat together the milk, oil and egg whites. Pour this mixture into the dry ingredients and stir until well blended. Add the bananas and raisins, and stir until combined. Spread the batter evenly in the pan and bake for 45 minutes, or until the cake is lightly browned and pulls away from the sides of the pan. Cool the cake in the pan on a rack for at least 10 minutes, then cut it into 8 squares and serve.

Makes 8 servings

BERRY-CHEESE DIP WITH PITA SCOOPS

A half cup of cream cheese contains 125 milligrams of cholesterol and 25 milligrams of saturated fat; the same quantity of lowfat cottage cheese has just five milligrams of cholesterol and less than a gram of saturated fat.

CALORIES per serving	180
75% Carbohydrate	35 g
16% Protein	7 g
9% Fat	2 g
CALCIUM	40 mg
IRON	1 mg
SODIUM	298 mg

1 1/2 cups fresh or unsweetened
  frozen raspberries or
  strawberries, thawed
1 tablespoon light brown sugar
1 banana

1/2 cup lowfat cottage
  cheese (1%)
Four 1-ounce pita breads
1 tablespoon toasted
  sesame seeds

Combine the berries and sugar in a food processor or blender and process until puréed. Strain the purée into a small bowl, then return 1/4 cup of it to the food processor. Cover and refrigerate the remaining purée. Peel and quarter the banana. For the dip, add the banana and cottage cheese to the food processor, and process until smooth. Transfer the dip to a small serving bowl, cover it and refrigerate until ready to serve.

Preheat the broiler. Split each pita bread to form 2 rounds, then cut each round into quarters and spread them on a baking sheet. Toast the pita triangles under the broiler for 3 minutes on each side, or just until lightly browned. Meanwhile, pour the reserved raspberry purée on top of the dip and swirl it with a knife, then sprinkle the dip with sesame seeds. Place the bowl of dip in the middle of a platter, surround it with the pita scoops and serve.

Makes 4 servings

PROP CREDITS

Cover: woman's (left) and child's clothing–Macy's, New York City, woman's top (right)–The Gap, New York City, shoes–Nike, Inc., Beaverton, Ore.; page 6: men's clothing–The Gap, New York City, woman's top (right)–The Gap, New York City, woman's (left) and child's clothing–Macy's, New York City, shoes–Nike, Inc., Beaverton, Ore.; page 8: top–The Gap, New York City; pages 14-27: furniture–The Door Store, New York City, rug–ABC International Design Rugs, Inc., New York City, leotard and tights–Macy's, New York City; pages 28-47: crib and accessories–Lewis of London, New York City, rug–ABC International Design Rugs, Inc., New York City, ottoman–The Door Store, New York City, leotard and tights–Macy's, New York City, playsuit–Greenstones & Cie, New York City; page 48: sweatshirt–The Gap, New York City, polo shirt–Macy's, New York City; pages 54-73: child's clothing–Macy's, New York City, man's clothing–Tultex, Inc., Martinsville, Va., shoes–Nike, Inc., Beaverton, Ore.; pages 74-75: clothing–Macy's, New York City, shoes–Nike, Inc., Beaverton, Ore.; pages 76-81: sweatshirt–Macy's, New York City, shoes–Nike, Inc., Beaverton, Ore.; pages 82-85: clothing–Macy's, New York City, shoes–Nike, Inc., Beaverton, Ore.; pages 86-87: boy's clothing–Macy's, New York City, girl's sweatshirt–Macy's, New York City, shoes–Nike, Inc., Beaverton, Ore.; page 88: man's clothing–The Gap, New York City, woman's clothing–Macy's, New York City; pages 94-97: clothing–Macy's, New York City, shoes–Nautilus Athletic Footwear, Inc., Greenville, S.C., rug–ABC International Design Rugs, Inc., New York City; pages 98-111: clothing–Jockey International, Kenosha, Wis., rug–ABC International Design Rugs, Inc., New York City; pages 112-121: clothing–Macy's, New York City, shoes–Nautilus Athletic Footwear, Inc., Greenville, S.C., rug–ABC International Design Rugs, Inc., New York City; page 128: plate–Thaxton & Co., New York City; page 131: stainless-steel tureen–Sointu, New York City; page 134: serving utensils and glass plates–Pottery Barn, New York City; bowl–Thaxton & Co., New York City; page 138: sorbet glasses–Conran's, New York City; page 140: glasses and pitcher–Thaxton & Co., New York City, flower holders–Pottery Barn, New York City.

ACKNOWLEDGMENTS

All cosmetics and grooming products supplied by Clinique Labs, Inc., New York City

Nutrition analysis provided by Hill Nutrition Associates, Fayetteville, N.Y.

Off-camera warm-up equipment: rowing machine supplied by Precor USA, Redmond, Wash.; Tunturi stationary bicycle supplied by Amerec Corp., Bellevue, Wash.

Washing machine and dryer supplied by White-Westinghouse, Columbus, Ohio

Index prepared by Ian Tucker

Production by Giga Communications

Photo stylists: exercise, Laurie Jean Beck; food, Adrienne Abseck

PHOTOGRAPHY CREDITS

Exercise photographs by Andrew Eccles; food photographs by Steven Mays, Rebus, Inc.

ILLUSTRATION CREDITS

Pages 11 and 51, illustrations: Phil Scheuer; page 91, illustration: David Flaherty.

Time-Life Books Inc. offers a wide range of fine recordings, including a Rock 'n' Roll Era *series. For subscription information, call 1-800-621-7026, or write TIME-LIFE MUSIC, P. O. Box C-32068; Richmond, Virginia 23261-2068.*

INDEX